D1085166

THE HAMLYN LECTURES
FIFTIETH SERIES

FREEDOM, LAW
AND JUSTICE

AUSTRALIA
LBC Information Services—Sydney

CANADA and USA
Carswell—Toronto

NEW ZEALAND
Brooker's—Auckland

SINGAPORE and MALAYSIA
Sweet & Maxwell Asia—Singapore and Kuala Lumpur

FREEDOM, LAW AND JUSTICE

by

THE RIGHT HONOURABLE
LORD JUSTICE SEDLEY

Published under the auspices of
THE HAMLYN TRUST

LONDON
SWEET & MAXWELL
1999

Published in 1999 by Sweet & Maxwell Limited of
100 Avenue Road, Swiss Cottage,
London NW3 3PF
Typeset by J&L Composition Ltd, Filey, North Yorkshire
Printed in England by
Clays Ltd, St Ives plc

No natural forests were destroyed to make this product;
only farmed timber was used and replanted

A CIP catalogue record for this book is available from the British Library

ISBN 0 421 680806(HB)
0 421 680903 (PB)

TABLE OF CONTENTS

THE HAMLYN LECTURES

The Hamlyn Lectures

The Hamlyn Lectures

THE HAMLYN TRUST

The Hamlyn Trust owes its existence to the will of the late Miss Emma Warburton Hamlyn of Torquay, who died in 1941 at the age of 80. She came of an old and well-known Devon family. Her father, William Bussell Hamlyn, practised in Torquay as a solicitor and J.P. for many years, and it seems likely that Miss Hamlyn founded the trust in his memory. Emma Hamlyn was a woman of strong character, intelligent and cultured, well-versed in literature, music and art, and a lover of her country. She travelled extensively in Europe and Egypt, and apparently took considerable interest in the law and ethnology of the countries and cultures that she visited. An account of Miss Hamlyn by Dr Chantal Stebbings of the University of Exeter may be found, under the title "The Hamlyn Legacy", in volume 42 of the published lectures.

Miss Hamlyn bequeathed the residue of her estate on trust in terms which it seems were her own. The wording was though to be vague and the will was taken to the Chancery Division of the High Court, which in November 1948 approved a Scheme for the administration of the trust. Paragraph 3 of the Scheme, which closely follows Miss Hamlyn's own wording, is as follows:

> "The object of the charity is the furtherance by lectures or otherwise among the Common People of the United Kingdom of Great Britain and Northern Ireland of the knowledge of the Comparative Jurisprudence and Ethnology of the Chief European countries including the United Kingdom, and the circumstances of the growth of such jurisprudence to the Intent that the Common People of the United Kingdom may realise the privileges which in law and custom they enjoy in comparison with other European Peoples and realising and appreciating such privileges may recognise the responsibilities and obligations attaching to them."

The Trustees are to include the Vice-Chancellor of the University of Exeter, representatives of the Universities of London, Leeds, Glasgow, Belfast and Wales and persons co-opted. At present there are nine Trustees:

From the outset it was decided that the Trust's objects could best
be achieved by means of an annual course of public lectures of
outstanding interest and quality by eminent Lecturers, and by
their subsequent publication and distribution to a wider audience. The first of these Lectures were delivered by the Rt Hon.
Lord Justice Denning (as he then was) in October and November
1949.

A complete list of the Lectures may be found on pages vi–ix.
In addition, in recent years the Trustees have established a small
grant scheme to provide financial support for projects designed
to further public understanding of the law. To mark the Golden
Jubilee of the Trust, they also made four 50th Anniversary
Awards. The recipients were: Coatbridge CAB, North Lanark-
shire; Legal Services Agency Ltd., Glasgow; Liberty, London;
and the Centre for Criminal Justice Studies of the University of
Leeds. All of these projects, in various ways, disseminate knowledge or promote a wider understanding of the law among the
general public of the United Kingdom. Further information
relating to these projects is available from the Trustees.

The 50th series of Lectures, with due deference to both Miss
Hamlyn and Lord Denning, was delivered in the West Country
by The Hon. Mr. Justice Sedley (as he then was) on successive
Thursdays in November 1998. The first lecture was given in the
University of Southampton, the second in the University of
Bristol, and the third and final in the University of Exeter.

March 1999   **JOHN BRIDGE**
                                          Chairman of the Trustees

PREFACE

These, the 1998 Hamlyn Lectures, are the 50th in an unbroken series. The honour of being asked to deliver them was made more daunting by the fact that the author of the first Hamlyn Lectures, Lord Denning, was now in his hundredth year. Denning's 1949 lectures were an instant classic: so much so that the great line we have learned to attribute to Lord Mansfield in *Somersett's Case*—"The air of England is too pure for any slave to breathe: let the black go free"—which appears in no contemporary report of the judgment, seems to have originated there.

At the Trustees' suggestion I have taken as my theme a variant of Lord Denning's subject, "Freedom under the Law", and devoted one lecture to freedom, one to law and one to justice. I cannot claim to have advanced a new or comprehensive theory of any of these, but I hope that the three papers offer a cohesive approach to some of the major issues which English law faces as it approaches a new century in a new ambience of human rights. They argue that the concept of a free society, a society governed by laws made democratically and administered justly, as the matrix of individual freedoms is a critical part of our historical legacy; that precisely because it is not law's task to redistribute power, its central concern needs to be with the abuse of power, whether public or private; and that justice has to be sought not in crystalline outcomes but by the principled negotiation through law of interests which may be no less legitimate for want of the status of tabulated rights. If a substantive boat is being pushed out, it is in the second lecture, which argues for a symbiotic development of public and private law in the human rights culture which will mark the transition into the new century.

We know now that when Lord Denning's lectures were published in 1949, the Lord Chancellor, Viscount Jowitt, wrote to him: "I always hold my thumbs, as the children say, when I hear that a judge has written a book"—Jowitt was probably remembering Lord Hewart's fulminations in *The New Despotism* 20 years earlier—"and I am old-fashioned enough to think that the less they write the better it is for all concerned. I feel this for two reasons. Firstly because a judge is so likely to commit himself to some proposition of law with regard to which he has not had the advantage of hearing argument and which may therefore be too widely stated, and secondly because he may so easily slip over the borderline which separates controversial and uncontroversial matters." The first of Lord Jowitt's reasons still holds good—but while it is a reason for keeping extra-judicial thinking separate from judicial decision-making, it is not, I think, a reason for silence. If part of the common law's problem is that it is reactive, it may be that some proactive thinking by its practitioners will help it to develop in principled ways. The second of Lord Jowitt's reasons has gone with the Kilmuir rules which sought to keep judges away from any risk of public controversy. While I hope that nothing in these lectures is partisan, I would be sorry to think that they were entirely uncontroversial. Justice, as Lord Atkin remarked, is not a clois-tered virtue, and modern judges ought to have something to contribute to public discussion of issues of freedom, of law and of justice.

In working on these lectures I have had much kind help and have incurred many debts of gratitude, not least to Professor Desmond Greer, the then Chairman of the Hamlyn Trustees, who organised the series and piloted me through it. Most particu-larly, I was able to work on the second lecture during August 1998 in New Zealand, thanks to the generosity of the Law Faculty of Victoria University of Wellington and the support of the British Council, which provided for my accommodation and sponsored a dry run of the lecture before a distinguished audience. Janet Maclean of the New Zealand Institute of Public Law, Justices Sir Kenneth Keith and Ted Thomas of the New Zealand Court of Appeal, and its former President, now Lord Cooke of Thorndon, went far beyond the call of duty to make my visit an agreeable and fruitful one. The hospitality of the Governor-General, Sir Michael Hardie Boys, and of the High Commissioner, Martin Williams, as well as of my fellow judges in Wellington and Auckland, set the seal on a productive stay. I have also had much stimulation and support from judicial and academic colleagues in Canada, where I spent some time in October 1997 as Laskin Visiting Professor at Osgoode Hall Law School. It is for these reasons, and because in December 1998 I was invited by Interights to a human rights colloquium in Bangalore where I had the privilege of talking with some of the Indian judges who have contributed to the flowering of human rights jurisprudence in South Asia, that my examples and anno-tations tend to be drawn from these rather than other parts of the common law world.

Preface

Among the many colleagues and friends to whom I have turned for advice (though they bear no responsibility for what I have made of it), let me mention and thank Anthony Bradley, Andrew Butler, Gerry Cohen, John Evans, Douglas Hay, Janet Maclean, Basil Markesinis, Alan Rusbridger, Steven Rose, David Sedley, Amartya Sen, Antony Shaw, Jennifer Temkin and Michael Taggart. I also owe a debt of gratitude fo the three law schools which generously hosted the lectures: Southampton University, in Lord Denning's county of Hampshire, where Professor Nick Wikeley, with Professor Jeremy Cooper of the Southampton Institute, arranged for the first lecture to be delivered; Bristol University, where Professor Rebecca Bailey-Harris kindly introduced my second paper; and Exeter University, in Miss Hamlyn's own county of Devon, where Professor John Bridge, of the Hamlyn Trustees, arranged a memorable final occasion with the help of the Hamlyn Lectures' dependable publishers, Sweet and Maxwell.

I hope above all that the students who filled the lecture theatres will have carried away some sense of the possibilities that lie ahead for law and for justice—without which there can be no meaningful freedom.

Stephen Sedley
Royal Courts of Justice
London
January 1999

1. The Free Individual and the Free Society

Is law the natural enemy of freedom? Is freedom, even in a liberal democracy, simply the silence that remains when law has finished speaking?

The view that it is so, whatever judges might say in public lectures, was unforgettably advanced by A.P. Herbert in his imagined High Court judgment[1] on Mr Albert Haddock's appeal against his conviction by a London stipendiary magistrate for having jumped off Hammersmith Bridge during a regatta. The Lord Chief Justice said:

> "It is a principle of English law that a person who appears in a police court has done something undesirable."

Mr Haddock, he accepted, had an answer to all six charges laid against him; but, he went on,

> ". . . in addition to these particular answers, all of which in my judgment have substance, the appellant made the general answer that this was a free country and a man can do what he likes if he does nobody any harm . . . It cannot be too clearly understood that this is *not* a free country, and it will be an evil day for the legal profession when it is. The citizens of London must realise that there is almost nothing they are allowed to do. Prima facie all actions are illegal, if not by Act of Parliament, by Order in Council; and if not by Order in Council, by departmental or police regulations or bylaws. They may not eat where they like, drink where they like, walk where they like, drive where they like, sing where they like or sleep where they like."

Mr Haddock's defence had been that he had jumped off the bridge for fun. The Lord Chief Justice continued:

1 *R. V. Haddock: Is it a Free Country?* in A.P. Herbert, *Uncommon Law* (1935), p. 24. For examples of the continuing resonance of Herbert's critique, see Sir Geoffrey Howe Q.C., *Too Much Law?* (1978), quoting Tacitus: "The more corrupt the republic, the more numerous its laws"; Sir. C. Staughton, "Too Much Law" *Arbitration* (1998), Vol. 64, p. 200, quoting Grant Gilmore: "In hell there will be nothing but law, and due process will be meticulously observed".

"And least of all, may they do unusual actions for fun. We are not here for fun. There is no reference to fun in any Act of Parliament. If anything is said in this court to encourage a belief that Englishmen are entitled to jump off bridges for their own amusement the next thing to go will be the Constitution."

Herbert's individualistic view of freedom, and of the law's endless pettifogging interference with it, is the libertarian view which informs both of Isaiah Berlin's celebrated versions of liberty, the positive and negative.[2] The "positive" version—personal autonomy—and the negative—freedom from interference—are, as Berlin admits, conceptually not very different, but historically, he suggests, they have become polarised. The autonomous individual visualised in the positive concept of liberty has become someone who knows not only what is good for him or herself but what is good for the rest of us. It is to such individuals that Berlin ascribes the tyrannies of the twentieth century. But the seeker of negative freedom, he argues, wants simply to be left alone, subject only to the minimum of social regulation. Such a person, Berlin contends, is truly free.

Leaving aside the large question of what *is* the minimum of social regulation, there is a sharp and simple critique of this negative concept of liberty. It is that the absence of constraint gives freedom only to those who have the means to take advantage of it.[3] The abolition of South Africa's apartheid laws has

2 "Two Concepts of Liberty", Berlin's 1958 inaugural lecture as Chichele Professor, reprinted in *The Proper Study of Mankind* (1997). I have some sympathy with Christopher Hitchens' remark in his review of Michael Ignatieff's biography of Berlin (London Review of Books, November 26, 1998): "The greatest hardship experienced by a person trying to apprehend Berlin's presentation of 'two concepts' of liberty is in remembering which is supposed to be which," Although I have used Berlin's dichotomy as a focal point because it is well known, the fact is that while his "negative" liberty is a recognisable construct carefully shorn of its political and social implications (see below), what he terms "positive" liberty is a comparably careful conflation of communitarian ideas with the political abuses of them which have marked much of the 20th century. Ignatieff in a paper given after Berlin's death (see *The Independent*, December 8, 1998) seeks to redeem Berlin's analysis by allocating the negative and the positive concepts dispassionately to liberalism and to social democracy: ". . . it's simply not the case that negative liberty means laissez-faire. It once meant much more in freeing men and women from superstition, tyranny and oppression . . . Positive liberty warrants compulsory primary and secondary education, compulsory taxation and transfer of income, public health." One wonders, however, how many proponents of negative liberty would let all these positive babies go out with the bathwater, and whether proponents of positive liberty would not advance an even stronger claim to the defeat of superstition and tyranny.
3 The critique is advanced by Berlin's successor in the Chichele chair, G.A. Cohen, in his paper, "Freedom and Money" (Oxford, April 1998).

removed the legal constraints on who may go and live where: in the negative sense there is complete freedom of movement and location. Yet—as the new regime is the first to acknowledge— until black people are economically and socially empowered, whether by prosperity or by state intervention, the shanty towns in which millions of them remain will continue to shrivel freedom in what is now politically and legally a free country.

It is because of the political arguments which flow from the two positions (or perhaps more candidly, from which the two positions flow) that Berlin's negative liberty has become associated with or appropriated by ideologues of the right, and the critique of it with or by those of the left. But libertarianism is not in fact limited to one end of the political spectrum; it characterises, as extremes tend to do, both ends. I shall return in the course of this lecture to what I believe to be the poverty of libertarianism; but I want first to consider what freedom should mean within a modern system of law. It has, I suggest, two distinct but related registers.

One is the hard truth—truism even—that rights without remedies are of little value. To possess a legal right of free speech or movement is of little value if you lack the legal means to vindicate it when others obstruct it; and legal means include both access to the courts and skilled representation in court. The courts in common law systems—and no doubt in other systems too—have historically been alert to the dichotomy of rights and remedies. As Chief Justice Holt remarked when faced with an early version of the floodgates argument in 1701[4]: "If men will multiply injuries, actions [that is, lawsuits] must be multiplied too".

To assert that negative liberty is like a right without a remedy is not, however, to say that either is valueless. The second register in which legal freedom sounds is a symbolic one, and symbols can have a mobilising power of their own. E.P. Thompson's celebrated study of what he called the moral economy of the English crowd in the eighteenth century[5] set out to unpack and examine the assumptions wrapped in the lofty generalisations of historians about the riots which peppered the later eighteenth century. Far from being bent upon crime and vandalism, Thompson showed, the crowd could frequently be seen to be

4 *Ashby v. White* (1703) 2 Ld. Raym. 938 at 955. The difference in date is because Holt's solitary dissent was not upheld by the House of Lords until 1703, when Raymond reported the full case. Recent experience in New Zealand has shown a similar judicial determination to keep remedies in harness with rights: *Simpson v. A-G (Baigent's Case)* [1994] 3 N.Z.L.R. 667.
5 See the eponymous article in "Past and Present", no. 50 (1971), reprinted in E.P. Thompson, *Customs in Common* (1993) Chaps. 4 and 5.

responding to a shared sense of legitimacy. This moral economy, he argued:

"supposed definite and passionately held notions of the common weal—notions which, indeed, found some support in the paternalist traditions of the authorities; notions which the people re-echoed so loudly in their turn that the authorities were in some measure the prisoners of the people."

In his later work[6] Thompson contended—in my view absolutely correctly—that legitimacy was one of history's major prizes. If it is so, it is because without necessarily delivering any immediate results, capture of the high ground of legitimacy can give a purchase on more concrete outcomes.

The most striking example of this in modern times has probably been the movement for civil rights in the United States. Black Americans had learned to see the Constitution as the property of white Americans, which was exactly how white Americans saw it. The Civil War had abolished slavery as an institution, but the amended Constitution had delivered nothing through the courts except the legitimation of continued racial segregation.[7] Yet a quantum leap was made when during the 1950s the civil rights movement claimed the Fourteenth Amendment, promising the equal protection of the laws, as its own. Under the pressure of events, rights lititgation began to deliver results for black Americans—imperfect and in many instances reversible results, for litigation rarely alters the course of history, but results which helped to consolidate a shift of legitimacy that is now an acknowledged element in the moral economy of the United States.[8] Can anybody who watched the television newsreels of black people forming patient queues before dawn to cast their first-ever votes in a free South Africa doubt that, whatever the new franchise was going to produce in terms of living standards, they were witnessing a revolution in legitimacy?

Is this law or is it politics? In the years around 1970, when I was getting started at the Bar, there used to be a demonstration about one political issue or another almost every weekend in

---

6 *Whigs and Hunters* (1975), chap. 10. His further proposition that the rule of law is an unqualified human good has to be examined in the light of modern experience of regimes which function strictly according to law, *i.e.* without arbitrariness, but whose laws are discriminatory and oppressive. The better view must be that the rule of law is a necessary but not a sufficient condition of a decent society.

7 *Plessy v. Ferguson* 163 U.S. 537 (1896).

8 For excellent studies of the background, see Taylor Branch, *Parting the Waters* (1988); Randall Kennedy, "Martin Luther King's constitution: a legal history of the Montgomery bus boycott" in 98 Yale L.J.999 (1989). The latter situates the legal processes in the movement's history.

London. Most demonstrators were good-natured, but some set out to provoke the police, who for their part did not always wait to be provoked. The inner London magistrates' courts in consequence had before them a steady stream of young people, most of them seeming to the magistrates to be in need of a haircut, charged with public order offences. Their defence was usually that they were simply demonstrating, and cross-examination of the arresting officer would sometimes go like this:

"*Counsel*: Tell me, sergeant, have you ever heard the expression 'It's a free country'?
Police sergeant (suspiciously): Yes, sir.
Counsel: What do you suppose it means?
Police sergeant: Never really thought about it, sir.
Magistrate: Can we leave politics out of this?"

As the millennium comes over the horizon, we shall find ourselves taking a new and hard look at such questions. The suggestion that freedom has to do with politics rather than law was never a sound one; but the passage of the Human Rights Act 1998,[9] permitting only such exercises of power as the courts judge tolerable in a democratic society, scotches it for good. Freedom is where politics and law both compete and interpenetrate. It is a word which means everything and nothing; a word, as Isaiah Berlin said, "so porous that there is little interpretation that it seems able to resist".[10] Yet it is both possible and necessary to look at freedom neither as everything nor as nothing, but as something on which societies from period to period reach a negotiated consensus. From such a vantage point it is possible to peer a little way into the future, knowing that whatever else history does, it cannot repeat itself.

The British consensus on freedom is still, in the dying days of the twentieth century, essentially the one arrived at in the course of the constitutional upheavals of the seventeenth. Like other hegemonic ideas it is under continual and often necessary challenge from within. Nor is it common to the states who form with us the Council of Europe and appoint the judges of its Court of Human Rights. And, like everything else, it undergoes its own slow forms of sea-change. But the legacy of the seventeenth century settlement by which we continue to live and be governed is not simply a culture of possessive individualism,

9 The Act received the Royal Assent on November 9, 1998, in the week in which this lecture was delivered. At the time of writing it is expected to be brought into force before the end of 2000.
10 "Two Concepts of Liberty" (1958) in I. Berlin, *The Proper Study of Mankind* (1997), p. 193.

though possessive individualism forms a strong strand of it.[11] It is equally, and perhaps more importantly, a culture of republicanism—of a society which aims not merely to be composed of free individuals but to be itself free.

Republicanism may sound an odd element to single out in what is still one of the world's most stable monarchies, but it is not. The head which fell to the executioner's axe on January 30, 1649 was the head of a monarch who claimed a right to govern with or without the consent of an elected legislature.[12] The head on which the crown was replaced on May 25, 1660 belonged to a monarch whose attempts to revert to the old autocracy met with resistance (little of it, it has to be said, from the judges) which finally toppled his dynasty. His heir finally forfeited the support of those who now claimed to represent the people and had to flee. The crown was offered to the Dutch monarchy by a parliament which had set out the terms of tenure of the throne in a Bill of Rights which denied the monarch any final powers.[13] The City of London, which had played a key role in restoring Charles II to the throne, now came constitutionally into its own, principally by being given the purse-strings of the monarchy. Although optimistic radicals who returned to England were swiftly sent back into exile, and although the dispensing power of monarchs took another generation to die[14], the day of autocracy was over.[15]

---

11 The phrase is that of C.B. MacPherson, originally in the *Cambridge Journal*, (1954),pp. vii, 560–568 but classically in his *Political Theory of Possessive Individualism* (1962).

12 The assertion that it was a divine right had ceased to add anything to the claim; the parliament side, the Levellers, the Diggers, the Ranters, all now had God on their side. The claim to divine sanction has been a perennial part of struggles for legitimacy, not simply in the ubiquitous episcopal blessing of armies and weapons, but from the dogged persistence of the Everlasting Gospel as a hedge-theology of peasant and artisan rebellion (see John Warr, *A Spark in the Ashes* (1648–1649), S. Sedley and L. Kaplan ed., (1992), pp. 15–18) to the invocation of sectarian Christianities to legitimate political and social conflict in Northern Ireland.

13 Bill of Rights, 1688 (I Will. and Mar. Sess. 2, c.2) "The Revolution Settlement set down in writing the conditions which had been tacitly assumed at the Restoration": Christopher Hill, *The Century of Revolution, 1603–1714*, p. 276. Thus the abolition by articles 1 and 2 of the monarch's "pretended power" to suspend or dispense with legislation was a re-enactment of article VI of Cromwell's Instrument of Government, 1653: "That the laws shall not be altered, suspended, abrogated, or repealed, nor any new law made . . . but by common consent in Parliament"

14 William III vetoed five bills up to 1696; all became law in the end, and he gave up. The last monarchical veto in British history was used by Anne in 1708.

15 ". . . the beauty of 1688 was that kings had been changed without the state collapsing, in refutation of Hobbes. The state was now different from, and more important than, the monarch": Christopher Hill, *op. cit.* p. 289.

The use by the restored monarchy of the royal prerogative to pardon wealthy criminals was stopped. Governmental boards were set up which began to professionalise public administration.[16] The first beginnings of the cabinet, bringing heads of departments together, appeared; though it was not until well into the eighteenth century that it could be said[17] that the king had ceased to govern through ministers and that ministers now governed through the king. The judges did initially less well. Once assured that their tenure of office was (as the Commonwealth had established) conditional on proper conduct and not on the royal pleasure, they insisted that they had a freehold right to sell offices in the court system; and the Master of the Rolls, who had been doubling as Speaker of the House of Commons, was fined for taking a large fee from the City to get it exempted from the imposition of poor rates.[18] It was judges like Sir John Holt, who became Chief Justice of the King's Bench in the year of the Glorious Revolution, who as time went by began to take the common law, and the constitution with it, into logical and principled paths on which ministers were not allowed to tread except on terms of equality with citizens.

The consequent partitioning of state power between Parliament, the executive and the courts has continued from then till now to be contested, at least at the margins. But it was within a generation that Holt, trying the great electoral corruption case of *Ashby v. White*,[19] is said to have been confronted by the Speaker of the House of Commons and his retinue threatening the judges with imprisonment for contempt of Parliament, and to have ordered the Speaker out on pain of committal for contempt of court—"had you all the House of Commons in your belly".[20] It is to this symbolic stand-off, of which the deference of the courts to Parliament's enactments is a central but by no means the only

16 The diaries of Samuel Pepys, often spoken of as the first modern civil servant, give a window on to this process.

17 W.R. Anson, *Law and Custom of the Constitution* (3rd ed., 1908) vol. II., Pt 1, p. 41.

18 This was Sir John Trevor, who in 1695 was impeached and fined (after a debate over which he himself initially presided) for accepting what was called a fee but what others then and now would have called a bribe from the Common Council of London to bring forward a Bill in the House.

19 (1703) 2 Ld. Ray. 938.

20 The story is recounted in the DNB entry on Holt, where it is said to be mythical. But like other myths it contains a truth. What is better attested is that Holt had earlier been summoned before the House of Lords for contempt for deciding that a man accused of murder, Charles Knollys, had a sufficient claim to the Earldom of Banbury to exclude the jurisdiction of the ordinary courts. Holt refused to account to the Lords for his judgment, and the issue was dropped.

element, that we owe the bi-polar sovereignty of the legislature and the courts upon which the rule of law within a democratic polity continues to depend.[21]

The civil war which made the settlement possible was fought upon a political agenda which postulated not simply the entitlement of individuals to be free of unnecessary legal restraint, but the impossibility of such individual freedom in a society which was itself unfree—unfree in the sense that the ultimate power in it was autocratic and therefore arbitrary.[22] To the reformers of the civil war period, discretion and prerogative were the antitheses of liberty [23]. The Court of Chancery, built upon the need to mitigate the rigours of the common law by judicial discretion, had become detested for the consequent unpredictability of its rulings. Like the royal prerogative it represented what was autocratic and arbitrary in the state. Yet it was not until the end of the nineteenth century that law and equity were fused, and not until the great modern flowering of public law that the prerogative power—by now, and for two centuries past, deployed by ministers in place of monarchs—was brought within the rule of law.[24] I shall look in my second lecture at the case for moving on down this road towards the juridical control of all abuses of power, public and private alike. Meanwhile the tension between individualism and republicanism is still vividly present as we enter a new millennium.

It was Machiavelli, the seminal theorist of republicanism to whom many of the major writers of the seventeenth century looked back, who insisted that "it is not the pursuit of the individual good but of the common good that makes cities great, and it is beyond doubt that the common good is never considered except in republics."[25] The modern economist and philosopher Amartya Sen, by his analysis of famine as a breakdown of distributive entitlement rather than as simple food shortage and by his demonstration of its link with authoritarian

21 I have developed this argument in "The Sound of Silence: constitutional law without a constitution" (1944) 110 L.Q.R. 270.
22 See Quentin Skinner, *Liberty Before Liberalism* (1998).
23 See Donald Veall, *The Popular Movement for Law Reform, 1640–1660* (1970).
24 *R v. Criminal Injuries Compensation Board, ex p. Lain* [1967] 2 Q.B. 864: the judgment which merits special attention in this context is the second judgment, delivered by Diplock L.J., which recognises the prerogative as the last unclaimed prize of the 17th century conflict and asserts the supervisory control of the courts over ministers who now deploy it in the Crown's name. The decision was followed in the later and better-known case of *Council of Civil Service Unions v. Minister for the Civil Service* [1985] A.C. 374.
25 Niccolo Machiavelli, *Il Principe e Discorsi sopra la prima deca di Tito Livio* (1532), II.2, cited by Skinner, *op. cit.* p. 62.

polities,[26] has not only consolidated one of the principal utilitarian arguments for democracy—that it postulates at some essential level a responsiveness of rulers to ruled—but has helped to demonstrate that Machiavelli was right about republics.[27] In the centuries between, democracy has moved from being a term of abuse, synonymous with mob rule,[28] to being so much the norm as to have become the claim of every state, however tyrannical. Though all democracies differ, all are based on a belief that by providing for forms of representative government a people can become, albeit vicariously, self-governing.

But in a world which has seen at least two murderous regimes, that of Nazi Germany and that of apartheid South Africa, voted into power (the latter, it is true, by an all-white franchise), we may no longer suppose that the ballot box is where democracy not only begins but ends; that since whatever an elected parliament enacts is the law, to command an absolute parliamentary majority is to govern with absolute legitimacy. A democracy is incomplete without the rule of law, because while parliaments can govern in the name and interest of majorities, it is the rule of law which attempts to bring majoritarian rule into balance with the interests of minorities – including the most fragile of all minorities, the minority of one. The fundamentality of the task is recognised in the judicial oath itself—to do justice according to law. But the rule of law for its part, while necessary, is not sufficient. Parliaments can require courts to administer

26 Amartya Sen, *Poverty and Famines, an essay on entitlement and deprivation* (1981). Sen's initial thesis was chiefly a critique of the theory that a free market would correct failures of distribution. His later paper "Freedom and needs: an argument for the primacy of political rights" (The Foster Lecture, reprinted in *New Republic*, January 10–17, 1994) taking in new data about China's colossal famines between 1958 and 1961, enlarged the thesis to include a convincing critique of authoritarian government.

27 Although Sen's thesis broke new ground, the link of famine with human activity has long been perceived. Archbishop Laud (no liberal), attacking the wave of enclosures which had followed the first general enclosure Act of 1621 and which government, in the absence of Parliament, was now trying to halt, said: "This last year's famine was made by man and not by God". Sen's thesis, that the cause of famines is not general food shortages but failures of entitlement within acquisitive and distributive systems, concludes: "'. . . the focus on entitlement has the effect of emphasising legal rights. Other relevant factors, for example market forces, can be seen as operating *through* a system of legal relations . . . The law stands between food availability and food entitlement. Starvation deaths can reflect legality with a vengeance." His reminder that in the Bengal famine of 1943 troops guarded warehouses filled with foodstuffs while people died of hunger is testimony enough to the social responsiblity of law. I return in the second lecture to aspects of law's relation to economic activity and in the third to some issues of inequality.

28 See Raymond Williams, *Keywords* (1976), pp. 82–87.

fundamentally unjust laws—again, apartheid South Africa and Nazi Germany come to mind. And, political executives can dominate compliant judiciaries, as happened in the former Soviet Union. In the end we have to come back to a society's consensus about what is on and what is off limits. This is not, I think, best described as a higher-order law[29] because it has no authoritative source and no forum or means of enforcement (unless these are henceforward to be found in the European Convention on Human Rights and its court). It is, rather, what we collectively accept as the limit of what is tolerable; and our sense of this continues to be a complicated weave of individualism and republicanism—of a desire to be left alone and a contradictory recognition that we need each other; of the certainty that there *is* such a thing as society and an awareness that it cannot do everything for us.

Our modern history has in a sense been a search for ways of accommodating free individuals in a free society, doomed to incompleteness by the contradictory nature of the two things but driven by the need to try. One way of bringing into sharper focus the relationship between the two is to question the simplistic version of liberty as something inhering purely in the individual and diminished in direct proportion to the quantum of law and regulation. It can be done semantically, in the first instance, by making a distinction between liberty and freedom. Let liberty (Berlin's word) stand for the simple absence of inessential social interference; and let freedom (Denning's word)[30] stand for those things which people are not only permitted but empowered to do.[31] The common law has at different times and places recognised both the symbolic value of liberty and the practical necessity of freedom. Where it has repeatedly fallen down is in being prepared to sacrifice the latter on the altar of the former.

Take eavesdropping. Before an adverse decision of the European Court of Human Rights[32] compelled Parliament to pass the Interception of Communications Act 1985 there was no law governing telephone tapping in the United Kingdom. Did this mean that individuals were therefore entitled to be free from covert surveillance of their telephone conversations, or did it mean that the state and anyone else with the technology was free to tap their lines? The law of England and Wales, it was held

---

29 *cf* Sir John Laws, "Law and Democracy" [1995] P.L. 72 at p. 84.
30 *Viz.* in the first series of Hamlyn Lectures, *Freedom under the Law* (1949), from which my present theme is taken.
31 The distinction is proposed by Jonathan Wolff, "Freedom, liberty and property", *Critical Review*, (1977), Vol. 11, no. 3.
32 *Malone v. U.K.* (1984) E.H.R.R. 14.

in *Malone's* case, had nothing to say on the subject.[33] The consequences were twofold. One was that there was a literal state of anarchy, that is to say an absence of law, in relation to telephone tapping. The other was that, precisely because there was no law, those with power were able to impose their will on those who lacked the knowledge or means to resist them. I do not believe that anybody in the United Kingdom now considers this to have been an acceptable state of affairs, even though we dumbly accepted it; nor that anyone would now criticise the finding of the Strasbourg court that the want of legal regulation violated the requirement of Article 8 that any interference with privacy must be in accordance with law.

What does a case like this tell us about the rather abstract questions of liberty and legitimacy that I have been considering? First, I suggest, it points up how issues of legitimacy tend to pivot on events. Part of the legacy of the long sleep of public law from the First World War to the 1960s and of the associated potency of local and central executive government was a silent assumption that public power was not open to serious abuse because the police and security services were answerable to ministers, and ministers to Parliament. None of this was true for the simple reason that nobody knew what to ask or when to ask it; the revelation that Malone's phone had been tapped was a chance by-product of criminal proceedings against him. Once the issue surfaced, as it proceeded to do in other quarters,[34] the whole paradigm of legitimacy began to shift—and to shift healthily in favour of the rule of law.

Secondly, cases like Malone's highlight some of the limitations of a negative notion of liberty. In the absence of regulation by law, nobody's privacy is safe because everybody else is free to invade it. Yet it is Berlin's governing principle, the individual's right to be left alone, which gives both the householder and the eavesdropper their claims—the one to privacy, the other to freedom of action. You can try to control the state by postulating public law constraints of reasonableness on its activities: though

---

33 *Malone v. Metropolitan Police Commissioner* [1979] Ch. 344 (Sir R. Megarry, V.-C.). It is not relevant to my present purpose to consider whether, either in the civil proceedings as they were constituted or in differently cast public law proceedings, victory might have gone to Malone in the domestic courts. The Vice-Chancellor concluded: ". . . telephone tapping is a subject which cries out for legislation . . . [T]he requirements of the Convention should provide a spur to action . . ." But it was not until the U.K. lost in Strasbourg that legislation came.

34 *e.g.* in *R. v. Home Secretary, ex p. Ruddock* [1987] 1 W.L.R. 1482; *Hewitt and Harman v. the United Kingdom* (1984) 38 D.R.53 which the U.K. settled after the Commission of the ECHR had declared the complaint of telephone-tapping admissible.

what can be more reasonable than eavesdropping on someone who is suspected of being, but cannot yet be proved to be, engaged in serious crime? But whether or not you eliminate the state you still have private surveillance to deal with. The only way to deal with it, as the most dogged libertarian must concede, is to legislate—an instance, therefore, of the minimal social constraint which forms part of Berlin's paradigm. But what form is the constraint to take? Someone's liberty—the householder's or the eavesdropper's or both—is going to have to be curtailed, and it is society through its political and juridical mechanisms which has to determine how.

This, it seems to me, is both the point at which the complexity of democracy and the rule of law begins to be displayed and the point at which negative libertarianism runs out of ideas. Majoritarian society may well have a strong interest in licensing its police and security services to keep a covert watch on suspects. Regard for the individual, on the other hand, prohibits merely arbitrary or speculative surveillance by the state. These can be balanced against each other in a well-drawn statutory regime. But what then about private entrepreneurs—inquiry agents seeking evidence of civil wrongs, or newspapers seeking evidence of public or private corruption? It is possible to include such bodies in a statutory regime; but the libertarian view, which tends to regard such bodies as private persons and to counterpose their interests to those of the state, is generally opposed to such a course.

I will be suggesting in my second lecture that instances like this illustrate the falsity of the legal dichotomy of the public and the private; but for present purposes the issue illustrates the void which negative liberty leaves where the nature of a minimal but necessary interference has to be debated and decided. The free individual, as an atom coexisting or colliding with other atoms, as predator or prey or both in a genetically or biologically determined world, can only defend his own space. It is the free society which can at least claim to accommodate the wants of all such individuals, weak and strong, good and bad, and to protect them by the rule of law from arbitrary interference with their autonomy. But the counterpart of a free society has to be more than a minimal curtailment of its members' liberty: it is, whether we wish it or not, a partial renunciation of personal autonomy[35]—the social contract which political theorists from Socrates' interlocutor Glaucon

---

35 This vocabulary is meant to draw the contrast with other forms of society which, lacking democratic structures and methods, deny or forfeit individual autonomy.

onwards[36] have postulated as either the condition or the explanation of the development of humanity as a species.

The measure in which individuality can be fulfilled socially, and the measure in which self-fulfilment depends on individualism, are questions which have suffused and shaped the major political movements of the last four centuries. They are not legal questions, but they inexorably affect the law—overtly in the content of the legislation enacted by successive parliaments, but also silently in the policies which the common law from period to period adopts or abandons. From Chief Justice Coke's invigilation of monoplies of labour to modern public law's invigilation of the propriety of acts of executive government, the common law has made it its business to respond to those of society's perceived needs which it considers justiciable.[37] My present point, however, is that whichever view of the proper ratio of social to individual power has for the time being been in the ascendant, our society has resolved conflicts not simply by adopting majoritarian solutions at the expense of individuals and minorities (though this has happened more often than is comfortable[38]), but by recognising that individuals and minorities have interests which are entitled to recognition and protection. It has been importantly, though by no means exclusively, the role of the courts to stake these claims. They have often enough fallen down on the job, from their capitulation to Charles I over the Ship Money[39] to the inability in *Malone's* case to find a way of controlling state surveillance. But, from Coke's refusal to let the King sit in his own courts,[40] to the award of punitive damages against the officers of state who used a general warrant to conduct raids in search of the authors,

---

36 Plato, *Republic*, Book II, 358b ff. There is, however, a selfish and perhaps amoral edge to this social contract, which Glaucon ascribes to the fact that the profit individuals could made by wrongdoing is less than the cost to them of others' wrongdoing: a view which would find favour with some modern law-and-economics theorists but is much less attractive than Epicurus' view that mankind's development brought about and eventually institutionalised an awareness "that members of a social group can best secure freedom from being harmed by a mutual agreement not to harm one another" (A.A. Long and D.N. Sedley, *The Hellenistic Philosophers*, Vol. 1, p. 134).

37 My next lecture considers this history more fully.

38 Two examples are *Liversidge v. Anderson* [1942] A.C. 206 and *Franklin v. Minister of Town Planning* [1948] A.C. 87.

39 *R. v. Hampden* (1637) 3 St. Tr. 825.

40 *Prohibitions del Roy* (1607) 12 Co. Rep. 623. Although I have in the past (see 110 L.Q.R. 271 n. 47) suggested that as James VI of Scotland he had become accustomed to doing this, the Scottish judges had in 1599 voted contrary to his command and in his presence: see Claire Palley's 1990 Hamlyn Lectures, *The United Kingdom and Human Rights*, p. 20.

printers and publishers of the *North Briton*,[41] and from the gradual outlawing of slavery when Parliament was paralysed by commercial interests[42] to the holding of a modern Home Secretary in contempt of court for deporting an asylum-seeker who had been granted the temporary protection of the courts,[43] the courts have also from time to time stood up for individuals against the abuse of state or private power. What earns the courts far less public approbation, though it is what they do far more often, is their upholding as rational and fair of a variety of governmental initiatives which are almost daily challenged in the High Court. It is sometimes forgotten by aspiring village Hampdens that the protection of good government is as much the High Court's job as the castigation of misgovernment. Here, in fact, as much as in the criminal process, is where the communitarian dimension of law is displayed.

It is this interpenetration of democratic will and constitutional principle which still characterises what political thinkers of the seventeenth century regarded as the necessary precondition of individual freedom, the free society. To a modern libertarian a free society may be a contradiction in terms; but to the people who argued and fought to put an end to autocratic and arbitrary government it had a very definite meaning. It is a meaning which is far from spent in the world which is about to embark upon a new millennium, but it gives no single answer to the big questions: what guarantees that the rule of law will also be the rule of justice?; what can ultimately compel majorities to accord respect to individuals and minorities? No two democracies have reached the same answer, and none is a complete or convincing one. The determinative powers of the Supreme Court of the United States have certainly not made the case for judicial supremacy. But it is a mistake to believe, as the Victorian constitutionalists have induced us to believe, that the United Kingdom is, by contrast, a kind of parliamentary autocracy in which everyone, including the courts, simply does Parliament's will. It is not merely that Parliament has twice in a generation introduced external and ultimately superior systems of law—that of the European Union and that of the European Convention and Court of Human Rights—into our own; it is that both historically and actually our polity is based upon a standoff between Parliament and the courts, each respecting the exclusivity of the other's sphere of

---

41 *Entick v. Carrington* (1765) 19 St. Tr. 1030; *Leach v. Money* (1765) 19 St. Tr. 2002; *Wilkes v. Wood* (1769) 19 St. Tr. 1406.
42 See "Law and Public Life" in M. Nolan and S. Sedley, *The Making and Remaking of the British Constitution* (1997), pp. 49–52; A. Lester and G. Bindman, *Race and Law* (1972).
43 *M v. Home Office* [1994] 1 A.C. 377.

jurisdiction. The courts will not, for this reason, adjudicate on the retionality or propriety of some of Parliament's more remarkable procedures (such as the ability of a single member—who may be receiving payments, albeit now fully declared, from a heavily interested commercial enterprise—to destroy a private member's Bill which otherwise has the support of the whole House by shouting "Object",[44] or to talk it out by the use of prolix amendments and filibustering); and Parliament for its part will not discuss the wisdom or propriety of a decision of the courts, however incensed or baffled by it members may be, or seek to curtail the jurisdiction of the courts or deny citizens access to them, however much it may resent the courts' intervention. This is the historic compromise[45] upon which the functioning of our democracy within the rule of law depends. It can be disrupted,[46] but at an eventual price which neither Parliament nor the courts have so far thought it worthwhile to pay, nor are likely to think worthwhile in the foreseeable future.

The new century, moreover, is going to see Parliament and the courts embarked upon a novel collaborative effort to patriate the individual rights set out in the European Convention on Human Rights. It is an enterprise which crystallises a number of the themes that I have touched on. First, it reflects a sense which has been growing throughout the common law world for the last half century that certain individual rights have a legitimacy which no legal system can ignore and no social contract can wholly sign away,[47] whether in an advanced democracy or in—as Mr Podsnap would have called them—less fortunate countries which we have liberally lectured about human rights in the past. Secondly, it has been accomplished through the democratic process by inventing an elegant mechanism—the

---

44 Objection in any form to further proceeding on a Bill converts it into opposed business for which ordinarily time will not be available: Standing Order 9(6); but for Government business a practice adopted in 1940 continues the Bill from day to day until it is disposed of.

45 I have given above my reasons for preferring not to regard it as a higher-order law.

46 I have suggested elsewhere that it *has* been disrupted in at least two significant respects in the last generation. First, by the effective abolition of habeas corpus in all immigration cases by the Immigration Act 1971, s.3(8) as amended by the British Nationality Act 1981: "Where any question arises under this Act whether or not a person is a British citizen . . . it shall lie on the person asserting it to prove that he is." This reverses the ancient principle that it is for the state to satisfy the court that a detention is lawful. Secondly, by sections 25 and 69 of the Social Security Administration Act 1992 as construed in *Bate v. Chief Adjudication Officer* [1996] 1 W.L.R. 814: see M. Nolan and S. Sedley, *The Making and Remaking of the British Constitution* (1997), pp. 62–63.

47 I return in the third lecture to the question, indicated here, of the relativity of rights.

declaration of incompatiblity—which preserves Parliament's legislative sovereignty but enables conflicts between primary legislation and the Convention rights to be identified and eliminated in accordance with the United Kingdom's treaty obligation to conform to the Convention.[48] Thirdly, however (and this is the reason why I have not bee part of the vanguard arguing for adoption or incorporation of the Convention during these years) the Convention itself is a document written in the ink of a particular moment of European history.[49] It was of course intended as a never-again response to the horrors of Nazism and as a barrier against the pro-Soviet Communist parties which were candidates for power in Italy and France. It was also, and still is, a statement of classic nineteenth century liberal philosophy, presenting the state and the individual (law and freedom, in effect) as natural enemies and the former as at best a necessary evil. Each article correspondingly begins by asserting a simple right cast in the "negative freedom" mould and then (except where the right is absolute) qualifies it by setting out the purposes for which the state may invade it. In this way it replicates the individualistic strand in the weave of which I spoke earlier. The republican strand is also there, in the permissions given to the state to invade or deny most of the listed rights; but it is looked on negatively, devaluing any notion that the state as a democratic entity may have a positive role in protecting individuals and enhancing their lives.[50] It is one of history's many ironies, and an illustration of its complexity, that the Labour government which helped to draft and which signed the Convention in 1950 was the government which, in creating the welfare state, had given life to the wartime consensus in favour of a society that cared for its citizens from cradle to grave; and that it is in the years since then—years in which the welfare state has become the nanny state and been given its cards, and in which individualism has become part of the common sense of electoral politics—that the Court of Human Rights has set about teasing out of the Convention a jurisprudence that places upon Member States a duty to take care of people.[51]

48 Human Rights Act 1998, s. 4.
49 A full account is to be found in Geoffrey Marston, "The United Kingdom's part in the preparation of the European Convention on Human Rights, 1950" (1993) 42 Int. and Comp. Law. Qly. 796.
50 The sole arguable exception is the right to education in Protocol 1, Art. 2.
51 I look more fully at the question of "horizontal" application of Convention rights in the second lecutre. For a striking example of the ECHR's capacity for assertiveness in relation to freedom of expression, see its decision in *Guerra v. Italy* 4 B.H.R.C. 43 that freedom to receive information under Article 19(1) might require a state to disseminate information that was critical to the enjoyment of other Convention rights.

What Lord Sankey said in 1929 of the Canadian constitution, that it is a living tree capable of growth and expansion within its natural limits,[52] is equally true of the European Convention on Human Rights. This is why the Human Rights Act, by patriating the Convention, promises a new and richer legal culture for the United Kingdom—at least if, as I have suggested, a free society is one governed not by a bare minimum of law but by as much law as is necessary to make justice possible. But it is also why the Convention is not, and ought for a variety of reasons not to be, the final word on the content or ambit of a justiciable package of human rights for the twenty first century. Whether or not the election pledge that the Act would be only the first step towards a home-grown Bill of Rights comes to fruition, there will remain an important role for the common law in filling spaces around the Convention rights.

It is not simply that entitlements which many of the world's poor would regard as prior even to free speech and association—food, for example, and shelter—are not to be found in the wording of the Convention; nor that other values prized by the common law—freedom from fear, for example—are not there either. It is that in the half century since the Universal Declaration of Human Rights and its progeny were written and adopted, the world has changed and our standards with it. We would, I think, regard the right to be free of discrimination on grounds which include race, gender, sexuality, disability, belief and opinion as fundamental to human dignity, not merely in the enjoyment of the Convention rights[53] but at large. I suspect that many citizens of urban societies would today consider a right to live free from fear to be a fundamental right—again bringing the state into the paradigm as protector rather than antagonist.[54] We shall need to guard ourselves against the risk that the Convention will be taken, in the way that lawyers are inclined by training to do, to be an exhaustive list of human rights, relegating other fundamental needs and values to second class status.[55] Both the Convention and the law need room to grow.

---

52 *Edwards v. A-G for Canada* [1930] A.C. 124 at 136.

53 See Art. 14.

54 This is by no means novel. Art. 2 of the *Declaration des Droits de l'Homme et du Citoyen* (1789) set out security alongside liberty, property and resistance to oppression as the four basic rights which society existed to preserve. In 1941 President Roosevelt, in a speech to the Congress, tabulated freedom from fear as one of the "four freedoms" (the others were freedom from want, freedom of speech and freedom of religion) for which the U.S. stood.

55 This risk is perhaps highlighted by the adoption by the Court of Appeal in *R. v. Ministry of Defence, ex p. Smith* [1996] Q.B. 517 at 554 of a sliding scale of scrutiny geared to the "fundamentality" of the right in issue. That the risk is

What is going to make the coming years full of interest is that while the process of growth will occur within the historic compromise I have spoken of between Parliament, the executive and the courts, it is the courts which are being entrusted by Parliament with a role which is both creative and responsive. Nobody can say how it will turn out; but the task will include, whether we seek it or not, a continuing evaluation and a steady readjustment of the relationship between the two paragons we have inherited from the epoch-making conflicts of the seventeenth century—the free individual and the free society.

not insignificant can be seen from the decision of the U.S. Supreme Court in *San Antonio School District v. Rodriguez* 411 U.S. 1(1973) that equal protection of the law—applied in other cases to tabulated interests such as voting, access to the courts and interstate migration—did not apply to necessities of life like food and shelter.

2. Public Power and Private Power

English law is entering what is certainly a new phase, possibly a new era. By passing the Human Rights Act 1998 Parliament has not simply added another statute to an already crammed statute book. Rather it has called on the executive and judicial arms of the state, and has in effect pledged itself, to respect the norms set out in a treaty, the European Convention on Human Rights, to which the United Kingdom has been a party since its inception in 1950. Despite, however, being one of the prime movers in the drafting of the Convention, it was not until 1966 that the United Kingdom gave its citizens the right of individual petition to the European Court of Human Rights, and it is only now that the United Kingdom Parliament has made the Convention rights a part of its domestic law.

Lord Denning, in one of the first judgments on the effect of the European Communities Act 1972, likened the Treaty of Rome in a striking simile to an incoming tide flowing into the estuaries and up the rivers of our geographical and political island.[1] The Human Rights Act deserves a different metaphor—perhaps that of a dye which will colour the fabric of our law except in those places where the fabric is impervious to it. This is because the Act, at least on the face of it, follows the New Zealand model of infiltrating rights to the extent that the statute book will tolerate them. We already have some experience under the European Communities Act 1972 of reshaping the language of domestic legislation—even mildly torturing it—to make it speak the words of European directives[2]; and we may well find that the exercise of doing the same with Convention rights is not unduly casuistic or offensive to our linguistic sensibility in the great majority of cases.[3] For the common law, for delegated legislation, and for administrative policies and practices, there

---

1 *Bulmer Ltd v. Bollinger SA* [1974] Ch. 401 at 418.
2 See *Pickstone v. Freemans* [1989] A.C. 66, *per* Lord Oliver at 125–128.
3 In a paper delivered in 1998 to the Franco-British Lawyers' Association in London, Roger Errera, Conseiller d'Etat, said that he had traced only two cases in which the French courts had been unable to make domestic legislation conform with the Convention. This may have in part to do with the laconic and open-textured mode of French legislative drafting. In Canada provincial and

is no such problem: they must all yield to the Convention rights.

Where, however, the Human Rights Act encounters primary legislation which simply will not accommodate it, the courts have been given a new tool—the declaration of incompatibility. Furnished with such a declaration, ministers will have the power to amend the offending statute by the use of "remedial orders". They will also, in a relevant sense, have a duty to do so because— and it is this which distinguishes the United Kingdom's situation sharply not only from that of New Zealand but from that of every other common law country with a Bill of Rights—the entire state, Parliament included, is under a treaty obligation to conform to the Convention. What remains to be seen is how government will respond to a judicial declaration of incompatibility with which it disagrees. Governments appear now to have no right of appeal to the Court of Human Rights in Strasbourg: it is only the aggrieved individual who may petition the Court.[4] Will government therefore respect the court's ruling whatever its reservations, or will it have to adopt the inelegant expedient of refusing to change the law and compelling the individual to take the state before the Strasbourg court for non-compliance, so that Her Majesty's Government can argue that Her Majesty's courts have got it wrong?

It would be pleasant if the unpredictabilities ended here, but they don't. One major imponderable is the measure of the courts' receptivity to human rights issues. There is no doubt that across the common law world the atmosphere has changed in the last two decades. We have seen the Supreme Court of India beginning to draw out of the once dormant constitution a

---

federal legislation has repeatedly been found incompatible with the Charter: see the comprehensive schedule in Peter Hogg and Alison Bushell, "The Charter Dialogue between Courts and Legislatures" (1997) 35 Osgoode Hall L.J. 75. This is, at least in part, because the Canadian courts, armed with the power to strike down, have declined to adopt more catholic canons of construction in order to avoid conflict: see Andrew Butler, "A presumption of statutory conformity with the Charter" (1993) 19 Queens L.J. 209. Somewhere in between stands New Zealand's experience with section 6 of the Bill of Rights Act 1990: see Michael Taggart, "Tugging on Superman's Cape" [1998] P.L. 266 at section 280–286; *cf* Paul Rishworth's early exhortation "The potential of a Bill of Rights" [1990] N.Z.L.J. 68 at 69–70. But Lord Cooke of Thorndon has said that he "may be wrong" in his dictum in *Ministry of Transport v. Noort* [1992] 3 N.Z.L.R. 260 at 272 that section 6 "does not authorise a strained interpretation": see "The British embracement of human rights", unpublished, June 1998. (The error, if error there is, may lie in no more than the choice of epithet.)

4 ECHR (as amended by Protocol 11), Art. 34. The former Art. 48, giving wider recourse, has gone.

striking series of social, economic and environmental rights.[5] In Canada, where the now forgotten Bill of Rights 1960 had sunk like a lead balloon, the 1982 Charter of Rights and Freedoms in the hands of a creative Supreme Court has transformed the country's legal and political culture. The High Court of Australia has discovered an unexpected batch of civil rights in a constitution which for almost a century had been thought to contain none.[6] New Zealand has established that the omission from its 1985 Bill of Rights of any provision for special remedies will not prevent the courts giving damages for violations.[7] There is no reason to think that the courts of the United Kingdom will be insensitive to this wind of change. But it may be a mistake to suppose that the success or failure of a rights instrument is no more than a matter of judicial inclination. It is going to be fully as much a consequence of how lawyers shape up to the task. If Convention rights are used simply as fallbacks where other arguments have failed, the Human Rights Act may well become devalued. Convention rights will acquire the throwaway status of *Wednesbury* unreasonableness—a contention so regularly used as a makeweight that in the handful of cases where it really might be relevant it provokes unwarranted scepticism. If on the other hand lawyers (especially those now coming through the law schools) learn to discern the viable human rights issues in fact situations and to argue these with discrimination and skill as organic elements of their case, the courts themselves will be helped to understand the relevance and purpose of the Human Rights Act and a human rights culture may begin to take root.

Let me assume the best—that the legal system will adapt to the new approach, and that judges, academics and practitioners will learn steadily from each other as time goes by. I assume it readily because I think it is the likeliest scenario. If so, I believe that there are two major tranches of jurisprudence which are going to demand continuing attention. The first, which I hope to look at in my next lecture, is the question of substantive as opposed to formal equality before the law. The second, which I want initially to focus on in this lecture, is what is commonly but misleadingly called the horizontal effect of human rights.

---

5 See, for a seminal instance, *People's Union for Democratic Rights v. Union of India,* Bhagwati and Islam J.J., May 11, 1982; published as *Observe Labour Laws* by the Baliga Foundation. *Cf* the 1996 Constitution of South Africa, Arts 22–29, which spells out a series of such rights.

6 See *Australian Capital TV Pty Ltd v. Commonwealth* (1992) 177 C.L.R. 106; *Nationwide News Pty Ltd v. Wills* (1992) 177 C.L.R. 1. I have commented on these remarkable decisions in "The Sound of Silence: constitutional law without a constitution" (1994) 110 L.Q.R. 270 at 276.

7 *Simpson v. A-G (Baigent's Case)* [1994] 3 N.Z.L.R. 667.

What it signifies is the proposition that it is not only the state but individuals and, importantly, corporations who are required to respect the human rights of others: in other words, that in the field of human rights the substantive division of the public from the private sphere is or ought to be immaterial.

This is certainly not the pure paradigm of rights from which instruments such as the European Convention derive. Historically such rights belong with the nineteenth-century liberal view that the state, at best a necessary evil, is the natural enemy of the individual. In my first lecture I looked at some of the implications for the common law of this too-ready conflation of liberty with individualism. The function of a rights instrument, taken on this premise, is to show the state a red light in its dealings with its citizens.[8] Insofar as the state is credited with a potentially benign role—a green light role—it is to be found in the exceptions which follow all but the absolute rights in the Convention: for example where the individual right of peaceful association with others is qualified by a limited power of restriction in the interests of public safety, public order and so forth.[9] But there is nowhere in the European Convention an articulated concept of the state as a repository of obligations which citizens have the right to expect it to discharge: obligations, for example, to assure so far as possible a life free from fear or a safe environment. These are not economic rights, which of course throw up questions of affordability; they are, no doubt, social rights in the sense that they are enjoyed either collectively or not at all; but that they would feature in any human rights instrument being written today is, I would suggest, beyond doubt.

Yet even accepting, as one must, that history (and a measure of politics) has given us in the course of the twentieth century a series of rights instruments with more to connect them with the nineteenth century than with the twenty-first, the question of the public and the private keeps presenting itself. Horizonality is a convenient portmanteau term, but the image it calls up is not really apposite.[10] It is predicated on a model of human rights as essentially a bottom-upward process, travelling in the vertical plane from individual to state. By way of contrast it posits a horizontal cross-flow from individual to individual. Described

---

8 As this paper, I hope, indicates, I do not accept that the sole role of public law is to show the state a red light. Like amber-light theorists I would regard public power as a necessity, not simply as a necessary evil. See M. Partington, "The reform of public law in Britain" in McAuslan and McEldowney, ed., *Law, Legitimacy and the Constitution* (1985).
9 Article 11.
10 Its immediate lineage is in the jurisprudence of the European Union, where a geometric image of the possible reach of directives is more apposite.

in this way, the two axes correspond precisely with the assumed dichotomy of law's public and private spheres, and the metaphor reinforces the sense that these are as different as any two dimensions are. But the reasoning which questions the division of the public from the private has nothing to do with turning Convention rights through 90 degrees. It has to do with the much more direct issue of how the state is to fulfil the obligations which individual human rights thrust upon it, and this in turn has to do with the nature and meaning of the state in the context of the Convention and the new Human Rights Act.

The Act is unequivocal in imposing its obligations on the judicial and executive arms of the state. "It is unlawful", it says, "for a public authority to act in a way which is incompatible with one or more of the Convention rights"; and a public authority is explicitly defined so as to include the courts but to exclude Parliament. It will mean that both the substantive doctrines of the common law and equity and the orders made by the courts must meet the Convention's standards. Now the common law at present possesses no tort of invasion of privacy. Article 8 of the Convention, however, says "Everyone has the right to respect for his private and family life, his home and his correspondence." This is straightforward enough when the threat to a person's privacy comes from the state: the court can intervene to ensure that any interference lies within the permitted exceptions. Equally, if one simply regards the activities of non-state entities as lying along a different axis, the court will be powerless whether the threat to privacy comes from the next-door neighbour or a transnational news corporation. But what then becomes of the court's own obligation to act compatibly with the Convention? Does it extend to developing a body of law which will protect individuals from all violations of their Convention rights from whatever source? Because the metaphor has become part of the argument, and because—for reasons I have given—horizontality seems to me to assume the very thing that needs to be debated, I propose to call this not horizontal but cascade effect.[11]

---

11 Any metaphor risks misleading, but Lord Cooke's image of "interweaving" the scheduled rights into the common law (*op. cit.*) is a valuable one. Geometric vocabulary might drive one to say that Ireland is the only common law country to have achieved complete horizontality: see *Meskell v. Coras Iompair Eireann* [1973] I.R. 121 at 132–133, *per* Walsh J. I hope to be forgiven for not using the German coinage *Drittwirkung der Grundrechte* (third-party effect of basic rights), which again suggests an artificial extension of the natural ambit of rights—in the language of the common law, a *jus quaesitum tertio*. Murray

A great deal may turn, under the new United Kingdom Human Rights Act, on the deliberate inclusion of the courts—the judicial arm of the state—in the general obligation to give effect to the Convention rights. This may seem an obvious requirement of a rights instrument, but the Canadian Charter does not have this effect: early in its life the Supreme Court held that its structure and wording were such that the courts were free to make orders which themselves violated the Charter.[12] Other jurisdictions, by contrast, including the European Court of Human Rights have validated at least the availability of a cascade effect by holding that the courts themselves, being part of the state which is required to assure the delivery of rights, may be under an obligation to take legal steps to prevent interference by non-state actors with a Convention right.[13]

Hunt in his incisive article "The 'horizontal effect' of the Human Rights Act" [1998] P.L. 423 postulates a spectrum in order to escape from the polarities of the geometric metaphor. An elegant exposition of the universality of rights can be found in the dissenting judgment of Kriegler J. in *Du Plessis v. de Klerk* 1996 (3) S.A. 850 at 914–915.

12 *Dolphin Delivery* 33 D.L.R. (4th) 174 (1985); [1986] S.C.R. 573. But see *R. v. Lerke* 25 D.L.R. (4th) 403 (1986) (Alberta CA), holding that a citizen's arrest was subject to the same Charter restrictions as a police arrest. This has recently been followed in New Zealand: *NZ Police v. Song Van Nguyen* (Wellington DC) July 21, 1998. See also *Slaight Communications v. Davidson* 59 D.L.R. (4th) 416 at 442–444 (1989).

13 *X and Y v. The Netherlands* (1986) 8 E.H.R.R. 235 at 239–240 (no. 29); *Plattform "Aertzte für das Leben" v. Austria* (1988) 13 E.H.R.R. 204 at 210 (#32); *Gustavfsson v. Sweden* (1996) 22 E.H.R.R. 409 at 435–436 (45); *Young et al v. U.K.* (1982) 4 E.H.R.R. 38; *A v. U.K.* (Commission, September 18, 1997). Similar conclusions have been reached by the Inter-American Court of Human Rights (*Velasquez Rodriguez v. Honduras* 9 H.R.L.J. 212–249 (1988)). The UN Human Rights Committee, in comments issued under Article 40(4) of the International Covenant on Civil and Political Rights (the basis of New Zealand's Bill of Rights Act 1990) has expressed the clear view that the rights of privacy and of freedom from inhuman treatment are entitled to state protection whether the threat to them comes from public or private sources (44th session, 1992; 32nd session, 1988). The New Zealand Court of Appeal has recognised the force of the argument, without so far explicitly adopting it: see *R. v. H* [1994] 2 N.Z.L.R. 143 at 147; *Lange v. Atkinson* [1997] 2 N.Z.L.R. 22 at 32 (Elias J. affirmed on appeal), following *Duff v. Communicado Ltd* [1996] 2 N.Z.L.R. 89 (Blanchard J.). Valuable academic comment on the possibility of a cascade effect of the Human Rights Act includes Sir William Wade Q.C., "Human rights and the judiciary" (Judicial Studies Board Lecture, 1998); Murray Hunt, *op. cit.* [1998] P.L. 423; Andrew Butler, "The NZ Bill of Rights and private common law litigation, [1991] N.Z.L.J. 261] and, from a more sceptical standpoint, Ian Leigh, "Horizontal rights . . . lessons from the Commonwealth" (1999) 48 Int. and Comp. L.Q. 57. For illuminating comparative studies see Andrew Butler, "Private litigation and constitutional rights under the 1996 [S.A.] Constitution—assistance from Ireland" (1999) 116 S.A.L.J. 77, and B.S. Markesinis, "Privacy, freedom of expression and the horizontal effect of the Human Rights Bill: lessons from Germany" (the 1998 Wilberforce Lecture),

There are convincing reasons why the courts might well consider giving a cascade effect to the Article 8 guarantee of privacy. The case for privacy legislation has been cogently made in a paper given by the present Lord Chief Justice, Lord Bingham.[14] He argues that the need is apparent and that none of the objections—interference with freedom of expression, difficulty of definition, the preferability of self-regulation and the alternative possibility of a common law solution—is convincing. Lord Hoffmann has advanced a separate and equally powerful case for a non-Convention-based common law right of privacy.[15] The *Guardian*'s editor Alan Rusbridger has also cautiously added his voice:

> "Is it conceivable that . . . there is a case for a privacy law, if drafted carefully and interpreted sensibly by a discerning judiciary? That self-regulation has frequently been a fig-leaf behind which we have disguised our unease?"[16]

The correspondingly strong case for a cascade application of Convention rights under Article 8 meets, however, what is both a jurisprudential and a psychological block in the mindset which allocates rights and remedies to a domain which has to be either public or private. It is this that I want to examine and, as will become apparent, contest.

Twelve years ago the present Master of the Rolls, Lord Woolf, delivered a seminal paper called "Public and private: why the divide?" He answered his own question with a convincing analysis of the need for separate sets of rules to govern challenges to public bodies and contests between natural or legal persons. In short, as he pointed out, there are requirements of speed and certainty which make it necessary for the rules governing public law claims to differ significantly from those governing civil litigation. Analogous arguments hold good for many other branches of legal practice. But to accept this is not necessarily

---

(1999) L.Q.R. 47. It is noteworthy that the cascade effect, doubted by Sydney Kentridge Q.C. among others under the 1993 Interim Constitution of South Africa, is now spelt out in the final version by section 8 of the definitive Constitution. The effect seems in any event to flow inexorably from conflicts between two guaranteed rights: see *Re J* [1996] 2 N.Z.L.R. 134, concerning a clash between a parent's freedom of religion and a child's right to life; and see ECHR, Art. 17.

14 "Should there be a law to protect rights of personal privacy?" (1996) 5 E.H.R.L.R. 450. See also Rabinder Singh, "Privacy and the media after the Human Rights Act" [1998] E.H.R.R. 712.

15 "Mind your own business", the 1996 Goodman Lecture.

16 Alan Rusbridger, *The Freedom of the Press and other Platitudes* (James Cameron Memorial Lecture, 1997).

to accept that there is, or ought to be, a comparable jurispru-dential divide between the private and the public.

Let me start with what is perhaps the most fundamental of all public law concepts, the notion of *ultra vires*. The process of doggerelisation which has turned this adverbial or adjectival phrase into a noun can stand as a symbol of its metamorphosis from a doctrine of company law into one of public law. The early attitude of the law to limited companies was that, once brought into being, typically by the exercise of the Royal Prerogative, they could operate as freely, and if they wished as capriciously, as natural persons. In tandem with this, the courts from an early date[17] developed a hands-off policy towards the internal affairs of limited companies, culminating in 1843 in the decision in *Foss v. Harbottle*,[18] forbidding the use of legal process by a minority of shareholders to challenge the propriety of what the majority is up to. There is sense in this, not only on Lord Eldon's original ground of caseload control but because the policy of the Companies Act 1844 and its successors was to permit incorporation at will, so long as it was on standardised terms with obligatory registration and disclosure, and thereafter to let the company manage its own affairs. Even so, the hands-off policy of the courts towards limited liability companies contrasts uncomfortably with their interven-tionism towards (if not all, then some) municipal corporations, culminating in the surcharging of the Poplar councillors in 1925[19] for attempting, *ultra vires* as it was finally held to be, to pay fair and equal wages to men and women on their staff.

Seward Brice, the earliest scholarly commentator on the *ultra vires* principle,[20] argued convincingly that it was the abuse of the colossal powers conferred by private Acts of Parliament on the early joint stock railway companies which prompted the courts to set enforceable limits to their powers. The birth of the doctrine in 1846, fully grown like Pantagruel, is to be found in the Master of the Rolls' judgment in *Colman v. Eastern Counties Railway Co. Ltd*, [21] holding that things done beyond the ambit

17 See *Carlen v. Drury* (1812) 1 Ves. & Bea. 154, *per* Lord Eldon L.C.
18 (1843) 2 Hare 461. The doctrine has had to be diluted to deal with the worst abuses, including *ultra vires* acts: see *Edwards v. Halliwell* [1950] 2 All E.R. 1064 at 1066–1067.
19 *Roberts v. Hopwood* [1925] A.C. 578, upholding the surcharge and creating the fiduciary obligation which remains central to local government law. The decision does not sit comfortably with the Court of Appeal's earlier decision overturning a surcharge on Westminster City Council for buying horsefeed from the highest bidder (*R. v. Roberts* [1908] 1 K.B. 407).
20 Brice, *Treatise on the Doctrine of Ultra Vires*, preface to 1st ed., 1874.
21 (1846) 16 L.J. Ch. 73; 10 Beav. 1, blocking the operation of the rule in *Foss v. Harbottle* in cases in which a majority could be shown to be taking the company outside its lawful powers.

óf the powers expressly conferred on the company were to be treated by the law as not done at all: were, in other words, null and void (one of the tautologies in which the vocabulary of the law is so rich). With the growth in the powers of municipal corporations and regulatory bodies the doctrine, intelligibly enough, became transferred to them. But the limited liability company, though every bit as much a creature of statute as the municipal corporation, was by the development of the rule in *Foss v. Harbottle* progressively cut free of judicial control, turning the doctrine of *ultra vires* into a rogue's charter by which a company could avoid liability by pleading its own want of power,[22] and returning much of company law to the arena of self-regulation. The process of "humanisation" of private corporations perhaps reached its zenith with the recommendation of the Cohen Committee in 1945[23] that the anomaly should be resolved by enacting that "every company . . . should, notwithstanding anything omitted from its memorandum of association, have as regards third parties the same powers as an individual"—a well-meant endeavour to stop companies repudiating their own contracts, but adopting a means which revealed just how far limited companies had been allowed to travel away from being statutory corporations and towards a quasi-human status.[24]

---

22 *Riche v. Ashbury Railway Carriage Co. Ltd* (1874) L.R. 7 H.L. 653. Brice's comment in 1874 (*loc. cit.*) was: ". . . the Doctrine of Ultra Vires is constantly cropping up in unexpected quarters, and manifesting its effects in an unforeseen and unwelcome manner. One of its first onslaughts was upon the time-honoured maxim of the Common Law that a man cannot stultify himself [n. *Beverley's Case* 4 Rep. 123b.]—that the lunatic, the fool, the drunkard, and the knave, who have made a contract, shall not subsequently repudiate the same by alleging that neither they nor their agents had at the time sufficient brains or authorisation to make it. This maxim the Doctrine of Ultra Vires soon demolished, and corporations may set up their incapacity whenever it is inconvenient for them to carry out their engagements. It next ran full tilt against the less rigid but more equitable principles laid down by the Courts of Lincoln's Inn. 'Who seeks equity must do equity' and 'Who comes for aid to Chancery must come with clean hands' are two of the most elementary principles of the Chancellor's jurisdiction. But the new doctrine refused to allow them to be applied to corporations, and after much wrangling it came off victorious, and corporations can now be relieved from Ultra Vires contracts, and yet keep the benefits thereof [n. with the exceptions and qualifications set forth *post*]."
23 Cmd. 6659.
24 The Jenkins Committee in 1962 (Cmnd. 1749) advised the more modest course of giving third parties statutory protection against rogue repudiations. The whole concept of legal personality recalls the episode in Anatole France's satire on the Dreyfus case, *L'Ile des Pingouins*, in which a short-sighted early missionary baptises the population of an island inhabited entirely by penguins in the belief that they are human beings, creating an acrimonious

Yet it remains the historical and jurisprudential fact that limited liability and the entities which enjoy it are entirely creatures of statute. They are not conceived of as public bodies because what they do is regarded as by definition their own affair, and courts of judicial review correspondingly take no interest in their activities. But this approach overlooks two major realities, one physical, one legal.

The physical reality is that there are corporations which now carry out functions that until recently *were* the state's, and others which deploy more power in their field of activity than the state does. For the former, it is difficult to see how a function ceases to be a public function simply because of a change in who carries it out. After all, private functions are not regarded as becoming public functions simply because it is the state which conducts them.[25] The rights and obligations of a plumber who is called in to fix the toilets in an office building will not differ depending on whether the building is a government office or a corporate HQ; whichever it is, she will be able to sue for her charges if she is not paid, and no member of the public, however directly affected, is going to have standing to question the necessity for her visit. Why then is the same not true, *mutatis mutandis*, of functions which have an incontestably *public* character? Modern public law has come to recognise that it is the nature and purpose of a power, not necessarily its source or its repository, which determines whether or not its exercise is a public function.[26]

debate among the saints in heaven as to whether the act of baptism has invested the penguins with immortal souls or is, as lawyers would say, *ultra vires*, null and void. Janet McLean has drawn my attention to the contrast between early north American jurisprudence, treating each company as a "little commonwealth" with corresponding public obligations, and the abrupt holding of the U.S. Supreme Court in *Santa Clara v. S. Pacific Railroad* 118 U.S. 394 (1886) that corporations were persons for all Fourteenth Amendment purposes.

25 The Human Rights Act 1998 by section 6(5) excludes the private acts of public authorities. For an argument that this need not exclude employment rights, see G. Morris, "The Human Rights Act and the public/private divide in employment law" (1998) 27 I.L.J. 293.

26 See Lord Woolf, "Droit public—English style" [1995] P.L. 57 at 63–64: " . . . it should be the nature of the activity and not the nature of the body which should be decisive . . . "; Krishna Iyer J. in *Som Prakash v. Union of India* AIR (1981) S.C. 212 at 219: "The true test is functional. Not how the legal person is born but why it is created." For a New Zealand perspective, see Janet McLean, "Contracting in the corporatised and privatised environment"; (1996) 7 P.L.R. 223; Michael Taggart, "Public utilities and public law" in Joseph, ed., *Essays on the Constitution* (1995). New Zealand has arguably led the way both politically (in corporatising and privatising public enterprises) and jurisprudentially (in developing an analysis of the consequences).

The legal reality is something which runs counter to the entire mindset that modern lawyers have absorbed through their professional education and internalised in practice. It is that, in spite of a massive body of doctrinal fiction, legal personality and human personality are two different things. The fiction that the law can invest an abstraction with the qualities of a person of course serves a purpose: to invest with legal rights and liabilities an entity to which the law has given an existence independent of the individuals behind it. But to call such an entity a person, albeit a legal as opposed to a natural person, is mere witch-doctoring to the extent that it pretends to invest the corporation with attributes beyond those which are necessary for its existence. This is of course why the illusion breaks down at those relatively few points where the *ultra vires* doctrine or some other branch of the law prevents a limited company from doing something that an individual could not be stopped from doing. But such points are not located consistently so as to assimilate private to public corporations; rather the reverse. True, a company is not entitled to spend its money without regard to its shareholders' interests;[27] but the generous leeway permitted by law in terms of directors' perks and corporate hospitality compares unhappily with the decision of Sir Peter O'Brian C.J. in the Irish High Court in 1894 that the cost of a picnic for the Dublin councillors on the occasion of their annual inspection of the Vartry waterworks in the Wicklow Hills should be disallowed and surcharged on the members.

> "I now come to deal with the expenditure in respect of the lunch. . . . I think it is relevant to refer to the character of this luncheon. I have before me the items in the bill. Amongst the list of wines are two dozen champagne—Ayala 1885—a very good branch—at 84s. a dozen; one dozen Marcobrunn hock—a very nice hock; one dozen Chateau Margaux—an excellent claret; one dozen fine old Dublin whiskey—the best whiskey that can be got; one case of Ayala; six bottles of Amontillado sherry – a stimulating sherry; and the ninth item is some more fine Dublin whiskey. . . . There is an allowance for brakes; one box of cigars, 100; coachmen's dinner; beer, stout, minerals in syphons, and ice for wine. There is dessert and there are sandwiches, and an allowance for four glasses broken—a very small number broken under the circumstances. . . .
>
> The Solicitor-General in his most able argument—I have always to guard myself against his plausibility—appealed pathetically to common sense. He asked, really with tears in his voice, whether the

---

27 See Bowen L.J.'s celebrated "cakes and ale" judgment in *Hutton v. West Cork Railway Co.* (1883) 23 Ch. 654.

members of the Corporation should starve; he drew a most grue-some picture; he represented that the members of the Corporation would really traverse the Wicklow Hills in a spectral condition unless they were sustained by lunch. I do not know whether he went so far as Ayala, Marcobrunn, Chateau Margaux, old Dublin whiskey and cigars. In answer to the Solicitor-General we do not say that the members of the Corporation are not to lunch. But we do say that they are not to do so at the expense of the citizens of Dublin."[28]

To take a very different and grimmer example, large numbers of people are the tenants, or the dependants of tenants, of small or medium-sized property companies. Most of them lack security of tenure and an increasing proportion are on short-term lets. If someone in lower or middle management decides for reasons of caprice or spite to refuse to renew the tenancy of a particular family, neither public nor private law offers any redress. Yet if the same were to happen at the hands of a local authority, judicial review would almost certainly be available. In other words, the assimilation of legal to natural persons has travelled well over the boundary between fiction and fact. Among its consequences is the ability of bodies—limited liability compa-nies—which owe their existence entirely to statute to behave as capriciously as an individual is on principle free to do[29] with, at present, uncontrollable consequences for some of people's most basic needs.

This is an issue which is going to become more acute with the introduction of a human rights regime into English law. Are corporations going to rank as persons for the enjoyment of human rights? In Canada, partly because of the phraseology of the Charter, the answer has been a qualified "Yes".[30] The European Court of Human Rights, to whose decisions we are enjoined by the new Act to have regard but not necessarily to adhere, has held that corporations rank as persons under the

---

28 *R (Bridgeman) v. Drury* [1894] 2 I.R. 489 at 495–497. The case is conclusive authority for the proposition that there is no such thing as a free lunch.

29 Antony Shaw has drawn to my attention G.B. Shaw, *Everybody's Political What's What* (1944), p. 44: 2: 4 "Mr British Everyman thinks that he is governed by two authorities only: the House of Commons, elected by his vote, and the House of Lords, which he hopes will soon be abolished, although it is far more representative of him, coming into the world as it does, like himself, by the accident of birth. Really he is governed by as many authorities as the Russians: by his trade union or professional association, by his cooperative society, by his employers federation, by his church, by his bankers, by his employers and by his landlords. Most of these have practi-cally irresponsible powers over him to which no responsible state department dare pretend."

30 See *R. v. Big M Drug Mart Ltd* 18 D.L.R. (4th) 321 (1985).

Convention. In New Zealand, section 29 of the Bill of Rights Act says expressly that they do. I no longer regard this issue, as I once did, as an acid test of the desirability of enacting a domestic Bill of Rights. The fact that corporations are not human, whatever the law tries to say, does not necessarily preclude their arguing for the rights of individuals in their own corporate interests. And in any case no amount of formal exclusion will stop them funding individuals to carry their Convention baggage. My point is the distinct one that unless they are brought within a cascade effect of the Human Rights Act, corporations will be getting both the penny and the bun: a multi-national news corporation will rank as a potential victim of human rights abuse at the hands of the state, able to complain loudly of official violations of its right of free expression—yet people whose privacy it invades in the name of free expression will be said have no constitutional redress against it. They will be left to scrabble uncertainly in the present patchy law of breach of confidence. I know of no principle of law or justice which can validate such a paradigm of rights. A cascade model, by contrast, will carry a flow of rights and remedies from the Convention through the Act and into the courts, and from the courts into enforceable forms of recourse to the Convention right of privacy, whoever is responsible for the breach.

So far so good. But Article 8(1), which confers the primary right, is followed by Article 8(2) which sets out a series of grounds upon which the state can justify an invasion of it. It starts: "There shall be no interference by a public authority with the exercise of this right except . . . ". A corporation, however large, is not a public authority. What are the courts then to do about the plain need for a free press to be able to investigate and expose serious wrongdoing, as at least one element of the British broadsheet press has done with conspicuous success in recent years? The answer lies in the cascade itself: although a corporation is not, a court *is* a public authority. To the same extent as it is empowered to give effect to the primary right of privacy it will be empowered to permit such interference "as is in accordance with the law and is necessary in a democratic society in the interests of national security, public safety or the economic wellbeing of the country, for the prevention of disorder or crime, for the protection of health or morals, or for the protection of the rights and freedoms of others". The elegance of this solution lies in the fact that it does not put the news corporation on a par with the state: the licence accorded to each is limited by what is necessary in a democratic society—a test which is likely to produce different answers for a police investigation and a tabloid stakeout.[31]

I do not want to suggest that this is at present more than a fruitful line of inquiry. The courts will have in due course to consider not only the questions I have been exploring but the significance of the omission from the Act of Article 13 of the Convention, which guarantees a remedy for every violation "notwithstanding that the violation has been committed by persons acting in an official capacity".[32] We shall also need to give careful attention to the composition of section 6 of the Act: does the inclusion of public bodies imply the exclusion of private ones? Alongside these high-profile questions we shall have to learn to handle Article 17 which, echoing the classic statement of Article 4 of the 1789 *Declaration des Droits de l'Homme* that freedom is the right to do anything that does not harm others, forbids the use of Convention rights to undermine the Convention rights of others. If this is not a horizontal or cascade effect, albeit negatively couched, I do not know what is.

I need to return from here to the issue I touched on earlier — the learned response of our generation of public lawyers that the *ultra vires* principle is the basis of all public law.[33] Historically

31 I am happier with this solution, in any event, than with the Privacy and Defamation Bill proposed by the Guardian's editor Alan Rusbridger. This offers a trade-off: a right of privacy, couched in the language of Article 8, in return for a *Sullivan* defence of reasonable belief to libel actions. It exempts corporations (and, more dubiously, partnerships) from the protective ambit of the right of privacy. But the right is also made subject to a public interest defence which includes "preventing the public from being misled by some statement or action of a public figure". This seems to take us back to where we started.

32 Whether this is a restrictive provision which confines justiciable violations to those committed by officials, or an expansive one which underlines that act of state is by itself no answer to a breach, it seems likely that the omission has been made by Parliament to achieve (among other things) consistency with the prohibition on disapplying incompatible primary legislation. Instead the Act itself, by section 8, gives the courts power to grant any appropriate remedy within their jurisdiction. This overlooks, however, the fact that there are many persons other than MPs and judges who, acting in an official capacity, can and arguably should give an effective remedy for violations of people's Convention rights. Francis Jacobs (Advocate General at the European Court of Justice) and Robin White in *The European Convention on Human Rights* (2nd ed.), pp. 18–19, reach the unequivocal conclusion that "Article 13, by providing in effect that it should not be a defence that the violation was committed by a person acting in an official capacity, presupposes that it cannot be a defence that it was committed by a private individual".

33 Among the growing literature on this topic, see D. Oliver "Is ultra vires the basis of judicial review?" [1987] P.L. 543; P. Craig, "Ultra vires and judicial review" [1988] C.L.J. 63; Sir J. Laws, "Illegality: the problem of jurisdiction" in Supperstone and Goudie ed., *Judicial Review* (1992); C. Forsyth, "Of fig-leaves and fairy tales" [1996] C.L.J. 122; D. Dyzenhaus, "Reuniting the brain: the

there is an apparent symmetry in the transfer from private to public corporations of doctrines of limited power during the years of the nineteenth century in which the corporate state began to take shape. Some of the leading decisions of the Victorian judiciary make it pretty plain that they were consciously setting about controlling the power of a state which was interfereing on a growing scale with an entrepreneurial society of such vigour that it was jeopardising the conditions of its own existence. But the truth is that judicial supervision of public authorities antedated by centuries this conflict-ridden growth in the machinery of state.[34] Equally, it is surviving, with if anything greater vigour, the disestablishment of much of the corporate state in almost all the world's developed societies. The reason is that at one level or another and by one means or another, by direct intervention or by devolution or by licence, states have to make a certain measure of provision for the orderly meeting of social needs. Whatever its current governing ideology, the state has no other *raison d'etre*. And whatever rhetoric of liberty is used, all but the smallest and simplest forms of human society need an ordered distribution of power if they are to function at all. While this is not a sufficient condition of the rule of law (it would, for example, include a dictatorship) it is a necessary one. The role of public law in this elementary scheme is not well or adequately described as keeping the state within the limits of its lawful powers: the metaphor of the state as a limited company breaks down when its powers and their limits have sometimes to be invented in order to be defined. What public law is about, at heart, is the restraint of abuses of power. It has been so since the earliest recorded cases, and it continues to be so.[35] There is in my view no other theory capable of explaining how, for example, the courts today have a supervisory jurisdiction over the exercise both of the Royal Prerogative[36] and of powers exercised by bodies with no legal underpinning at all.[37]

If this is right, one can come back to non-state repositories of

democratic basis of judicial review" [1998] P.L.R. 98. Reference might also be made to the officious backbencher as a parodic explanation of the doctrine of presumed parliamentary intent: see M. Nolan and S. Sedley, *The Making and Remaking of the British Constitution* (1997), p. 16.

34 The Commissioners of Sewers, instituted in the early 15th century, had by the end of the 16th century faced judicial review for acting *ultra vires*: *Rooke's Case* (1598) Co. Rep. 99b.

35 *Nottinghamshire County Council* [1986] A.C. 240, *per* Lord Scarman at 249.

36 *R. v. Criminal Injuries Compensation Board, ex p. Lain* [1967] 2 Q.B. 864. See n. 24 to the first lecture.

37 *R. v. Panel on Takeovers and Mergers, ex p. Datafin* [1987] Q.B. 815. In New Zealand see *Electoral Commission v. Cameron* [1997] 2 N.Z.L.R. 421 concerning a voluntary body with powers of censorship.

power with a different perspective. Some may be exercising public functions—typically the allocation of resources of basic importance to the whole population. Control of these can, of course, be expected to be governed by procedural rules which recognise the special public need for speed and certainty of decision-making, and even by rules of standing designed to exclude mere busybodies; but it can also be powerfully argued that the substantive law applied to such bodies ought not to differ significantly from that which is applicable to the state itself. Other bodies—the press and broadcast media are a prime example—will be exercising functions not of a traditionally state character but still of radical importance to large numbers of people. Where such bodies invade what are now to be the constitutional rights of individuals, I have suggested that the means may exist in the Human Rights Act to ensure that such invasions are either justified or stopped. But is this an unacceptably novel configuration of rights and remedies? Is it one which impermissibly conflates the private and the public?[38]

I ask the first question because the common law, like the god Janus, is for ever facing both the future and the past. As the great Scottish jurist Stair pointed out in the seventeenth century, statute law possesses the great virtue of certainty but the unavoidable drawback of rigidity.[39] The common law's great advantage is its ability to respond to change or to adapt to the unexpected; but if it does so in a baldly reactive fashion it risks destroying the stability which a society is entitled to look for in its legal system. So the common law likes to travel back to the future, looking constantly for precedents that will blunt the edge of the anxiety that it is sacrificing stability on the altar of innovation. Sometimes we get awkwardly close to Professor Cornford's principle of unripe time, with its axiom that nothing should ever be done for the first time[40]; but the search for precedent is never entirely cosmetic. It reflects the equal and opposite pulls of adaptability and certainty.

Is there then anything in the common law's past which prefigures this symbiosis of the public with the private? The answer is an emphatic "Yes". Two examples must do service here, drawn from the law of trade and employment. Lawyers still

---

38 Novel it is not: see G. Borrie, "The regulation of public and private power" [1989] P.L. 552; D. Oliver, "Common values in public and private law and the public/private divide" [1997] P.L. 630, and "The underlying values of public and private law" in M. Taggart ed., *The Province of Administrative Law* (1997) p. 217; P.P. Craig, "Public law and control over private power", *ibid.*, p. 196.
39 Stair, *Inst.* I.1.15: "But in statutes the lawgiver must at once balance the conveniences and the inconveniences; wherein he may and often doth fall short . . . " (quoted by F.A. Bennion, *Statutory Interpretation*, (3rd ed.), p. 783).
40 F.M. Cornford, *Microcosmographia Academica* (1908), Chap. VII.

tend to believe that, in spite of modern statutory controls, trade and employment are areas where freedom of action is the common law's universal groundrule. At common law you can sell goods and services to and buy them from whom you please. At common law you can hire and fire, take or leave a job, without anybody being entitled to question the fairness or rationality of what you are doing. Or can you?

Since the eighteenth century, perhaps earlier, the common law has set its face against unreasonable restraints on the free movement of labour and on the availability of necessary public services. Covenants, albeit voluntarily entered into, which restrict an employee's freedom to move on and take his skills and knowledge with him have for the better part of three centuries been subjected by the courts to a stringent test of what is reasonable— reasonable, moreover, not in the deferential *Wednesbury* sense that a rational person could decide to do it, but in the direct sense that it is in the court's own judgment tolerable on public policy grounds.[41] Similarly, a person who was granted a legal monopoly or who held a virtual monopoly of a service on which a section of the public depended was for centuries forbidden by the English courts to levy more than what the court regarded as a reasonable charge.[42] The doctrines of restraint of the abuse of private monopoly power, although for the present they have drifted out of sight in England, have remained alive and well in the United States.[43] They formed part of a complex legal regime for the governance of markets in a period (from the sixteenth to the end of the eighteenth century) which we tend mistakenly to regard as one of laissez-faire practices. During this period, first by statute but then at common law, the cornering and distortion of markets was caught by the now forgotten crimes of forestalling, regrating and engrossing: profiteering by buying up goods before they reached the market; by buying them up in order to resell them in the same market; and by buying them in bulk in order to create scarcity. An overt part of the rationale of these crimes was the preservation of public order, and the eclipse of them coincided with two things: the raising and garrisoning of armed troops all over Britain for war with France, but capable equally of putting down bread riots; and the acquisition of almost scriptural status

---

41 *Mitchel v. Reynolds* (1711) 1 P. Wms. 181 at 195. See Halsbury's *Laws of England* (4th ed.), Vol. 42, paras 21, 24.

42 P.P. Craig, "Constitutions, property and Regulation" [1991] P.L. 538; M. Taggart, "Public Utilities and the Law", in Joseph ed., *Essays on the Constitution* (1995). The doctrine reappears in the 20th century in the Privy Council's decision in *Minister of Justice for Canada v. City of Levis* [1919] A.C. 505.

43 See *Munn v. Illinois* 94 U.S. 77 (1877) and the articles by Craig and Taggart (previous note) *passim*.

among judges as well as politians of Adam Smith's *Wealth of Nations*[44] (an early analogue of the modern law and economics movement). But there was plainly, too, a strong moral component in the creation and prosecution of these offences, and none the less so for its eclipse by a different morality still familiar to us.

Perhaps the most striking modern concatenation of the public and the private has been in the law of what used to be called master and servant—employment law. In England much of its development during the twentieth century was bound up with the law of trade unions, because it was often members and officials, contending that they had been unjustly expelled from or dismissed by what were in law mere voluntary associations, who resorted to the courts for redress. In a series of cases running into the 1980s the courts, continuously reverting to earlier authority, developed and applied a coherent body of principles of natural justice which members and, importantly, office-holders could rely on to protect them from arbitrary action.[45] By 1970 the need for uniform legal protection of employees against arbitrary dismissal had become so apparent that the House of Lords[46] went as close as it could to introducing a right to natural justice into every contract of employment. Within a year Parliament had introduced such a right by statute.[47] But for the legislative intervention it is highly likely that the com-

---

44 See Douglas Hay, "The State and the Market in 1800", *Past and Present*, Vol. 162 (February 1999), pp. 101–162. The last major proponent of market crimes was Lord Kenyon C.J.; his main opponent was Lord Ellenborough C.J. who not only survived him but sat in Cabinet. See generally P.S. Atiyah, *The Rise and Fall of Freedom of Contract*, pp. 363–366; E.P. Thompson, "The Moral Economy reviewed" in *Customs in Common* (1991). Hay (n. 17) cites evidence of laws against engrossing and profiteering in ancient Athens.

45 See S. Sedley, "Public law and contractual employment" (1994) 23 I.L.J. 201; J. Laws, "Public law and employment law: abuse of power" [1997] P.L. 455; P. Davies and M. Freedland, "The impact of public law on labour law 1972–1997" (1997) 26 I.L.J. 311.

46 In *Malloch v. Aberdeen Corporation* [1971] 1 W.L.R. 1578. Decided in 1970, Lord Wilberforce said: "One may accept that if there are relationships in which all the requirements of the observance of natural justice are excluded (and I do not wish to assume that this is inevitably so), these cases must be confined to what have been called 'pure master and servant xases', which I take to mean cases in which there is no element of public employment or service, no support by statute, nothing in the nature of an office or a status which is capable of protection. If any of these elements exist then, in my opinion, whatever the terminology used, and even though in some inter partes aspects the relationship may be called that of master and servant, there may be essential procedural requirements to be observed, and failure to observe them may result in a dismissal being declared to be void."

47 Industrial Relations Act 1971, s. 22(1): "In every employment to which this section applies every employee shall have the right not to be unfairly dismissed by his employer . . . "

mon law would have completed the task itself. One of the most interesting aspects of the common law development was that it did not operate by implying terms into the contract: in the famous phrase of Byles J.[48] the justice of the common law was supplying the omission of the legislature. And it did so not by according a right to damages but by declaring unfair dismissals from office void—a remedy we have come to think of as distinctively one of public law.

It seems to me, therefore, that the moment of introduction of a human rights regime into the law of the United Kingdom, though millennial, is not arbitrary. It comes, of course, at the end of a long trek by a handful—of whom I was not one—of far-sighted campaigners led by Lord Scarman.[49] But it comes also at a stage of development of our constitutional common law when it is more possible than ever before to see how artificial the segregation of the public from the private has become in all but procedural terms. The old presumption that the Crown was not bound by statutes unless they expressly said so has become all but redunandant: legislation today routinely binds the Crown— as employer, as occupier, as contractor, as landlord—to observe the same legal standards as everybody else. The historic decision of the House of Lords in *M v. Home Office*[50] that ministers of the Crown are answerable to the courts for breach of their orders has restored constitutional law to a principled course from which it had been deviating for over a century; though we still have a certain distance to go in recognising the state itself as a legal entity.[51] By a fine irony of history, Dicey's well-known view that we had no need of a system of administrative law because everyone from the postman to the prime minister was governed by the ordinary law, is more nearly true now than it was when he wrote it—for our public law *is* our ordinary law, the common law.

In the historic decision of the New Zealand Court of Appeal in *Baigent's Case*,[52] Hardie Boys J. quoted some words of Anand J. of the Supreme Court of India[53]:

48 In *Cooper v. Wandsworth Board of Works* (1863) 14 C.B., N.S. 180 at 194.
49 Lord Scarman's 1974 Hamlyn Lectures, *English Law, the New Dimension*, make prescient reading. He called among other things for a new constitutional settlement with entrenched rights and restraints on the exercise of state power, and for a supreme court to handle constitutional and devolution issues.
50 [1994] 1 A.C. 377.
51 See S. Sedley, "The Crown in its own Courts" in C. Forsyth and I. Hare ed., *The Golden Metwand and the Crooked Cord* (1998), pp. 253–266.
52 [1994] 3 N.Z.L.R. 667.
53 *Nilabati v. State of Orissa* (1993) Crim. L.J. 2899.

"The purpose of public law is not only to civilise public power but also to assure the citizen that they live under a legal system which aims to protect their interests and preserve their rights."

My argument is not that the state is just another corporation, nor that (as was held in the great mid-eighteenth century cases arising out of the raid on the North Briton[54]) ministers should still be liable as private individuals for torts committed in office. It is that the rule of law, if it is to mean anything, has to embrace state, corporation and individual alike; that the law's chief concern about the use of power is not who is exercising it but what the power is and whom it affects; and that the control of abuses of power, whether in private or in public hands, is probably the most important of all the tasks which will be facing the courts in a twenty-first century democracy. The sea in which, as citizens, we all have to swim is inhabited not only by Leviathan—an alarmingly big but often benign creature—but by Jaws; and the law needs to be on the watch for both.

54 See n. 41 to the first lecture.

3. The Lion and the Ox

"One Law for the Lion & Ox," wrote Blake, "is oppression".[1] He was describing in his oblique way what Anatole France a century later described more brutally as "the majestic even-handedness of the law, which forbids rich and poor alike to sleep under bridges, to beg in the streets and to steal bread".[2] France's English contemporary Lord Justice Mathew made the point in more genteel terms: "In England," he said, "justice is open to all, like the Ritz."[3] The early Victorian poet Thomas Peacock, noting the unequal impact of the Sunday observance laws, said it in verse[4]:

> The poor man's sins are glaring;
> In the face of ghostly warning
> He is caught in the fact
> Of an overt act —
> Buying greens on a Sunday morning.
>
> . . . .
>
> The rich man is invisible
> In the crowd of his gay society;
> But the poor man's delight
> Is a sore in the sight
> And a stench in the nose of piety.
>
> The rich man goes out yachting
> Where sanctity can't pursue him;
> The poor goes afloat
> In a fourpenny boat
> Where the bishop groans to view him.

1 William Blake, *The Marriage of Heaven and Hell* (Nonesuch ed.), p. 203.
2 Anatole France, *Le Lys Rouge* (1894), chap. 7: " . . . la majestueuse égalité des lois, qui interdit au riche comme au pauvre de coucher sous les ponts, de mendier dans les rues et de voler du pain."
3 See R.E. Megarry, *Miscellany-at-Law* (1955), p. 254. As the *Oxford Dictionary of Quotations* demonstrates, the remark in fact has a long ancestry: see *Tom Paine's Jests* (1794): "A gentleman haranguing on the perfection of our law, and that it was equally open to the poor and the rich, was answered by another, 'So is the London Tavern'". A similar comment is attributed to Horne Tooke by Hazlitt, *The Spirit of the Age* (1825).
4 Thomas Love Peacock, *The Poor Man and the Rich on a Sunday.*

But the truth is that all laws discriminate. They discriminate between the virtuous and the wicked, between the permitted and the prohibited, between the taxable and the duty-free. They discriminate, too, on grounds which from era to era are taken to be so obvious that they do not even require justification. It was obvious that the right of all Athenian citizens to vote did not include women or slaves. Among the American founding fathers who proclaimed the self-evident truth that all men are born equal were several slave-owners. In this country until well into the twentieth century the unsuitability of women to vote, sit on juries or join the professions was regarded—at least by men—as too obvious for argument.[5] We continue to regard it as self-evident that the freedoms which we now regard as the birthright of all men and women without distinction do not apply to children. Our law, both common law and statute,[6] permits acts against children which, if done to adults, amount to criminal assaults. It was only in this generation, and only by the narrowest of margins, that the House of Lords in the *Gillick* case[7] closed off the enduring notion of parental rights as a form of proprietorship and put in their place a balance between the child's evolving autonomy and the parent's role as carer.

As to crime, it is not law—the argument goes—that criminalises some people and not others, but social conditions or personal choice that lead wrongdoers to do wrong. The law may be able to mitigate the consequences for those who offend through misfortune, but it cannot treat them as free of blame without forfeiting the very claim to even-handedness which its detractors mock. I will return to this question of the voluntariness of wrongdoing; but it is necessary first to say that Blake too was right. His was the age of massive enclosures and of the Game Laws when, as the jingle went:

"The fault is great in man or woman
Who steals a goose from off a common;
But what can plead that man's excuse
Who steals the common from the goose?"

Enclosure in England, like clearance in Scotland and Ireland, was the work of the law, but few poor people ever benefited

5 I have given some account of this embarrassing chapter of our legal history in the 1996 Radcliffe Lectures: see M. Nolan and S. Sedley, *The Making and Remaking of the British Constitution*, pp. 52–57.
6 Children and Young Persons Act, 1933, s. 1(1) makes cruelty to children a crime; but section 1(7) provides: "Nothing in this section shall be construed as affecting the right of any parent, teacher or other person having the lawful control or charge of a child or young person to administer punishment to him."
7 *Gillick v. Wisbech Health Authority* [1986] A.C. 112.

from it. Nor did the rich ever find themselves trespassing in search of game: they could pursue it on their own or their friends' land. The law which in form governed the powerful and the submissive – the lion and the ox—without distinction, was in substance a means by which the one could oppress the other and was meant to be so.[8] So undisguised an intention to discriminate by law between classes, genders or races may be a thing of the past,[9] but unequal effects of equal laws remain a living (indeed a growing) issue. Over 2000 years ago Epicurus pointed out that because of disparities of circumstance, justice does not necessarily demand the same result for everybody.[10]

It has been one of the great achievements of the last generation to recognise and begin to grapple with this snake in the legal grass. The United States' Civil Rights Act 1964, responding to the pressure of the civil rights movement, set out a simple prohibition on all discrimination on grounds of sex or race.[11] It was left to the courts to make this bald provision work, and they did so by recognising that discrimination could readily occur where, although the same condition was being applied to everyone concerned, it had a disproportionate

---

8 There is little doubt that the sole reason why the Georgian and Regency judges, who were otherwise active in developing new crimes, did not criminalise trespass by itself was that it would have made foxhunting impossible. This dilemma has plagued the law to the present day, resulting in the creation of statutory constructs like "trespassory assembly" (Public Order Act 1986, as amended, ss. 14–14C) and "aggravated trespass" (Criminal Justice and Public Order Act 1994, s. 68).

9 As recently as 1959 Parliament re-enacted in the Highways Act., s. 127, an offence of camping on a highway which could only be committed by a hawker or gypsy. It was dropped from the Highways Act 1980.

10 Epicurus, *Ratae Sententiae*, cited in A.A. Long and D.N. Sedley, *The Hellenistic Philosophers*, Vol. 1, p. 125. There is an important, albeit ironic, argument that inequality of treatment is not an exception but a rule of justice: see Pierre Moor, "Du principe d'inégalité de traitement" (E.R.P.L./R.E.D.P., Vol. 11, no. 3, autumn 1999), identifying three historical paradigms or "logics": "The first depends on the idea of the primacy of individual responsibility in relation to state action, which has to remain secondary: the principle of equality prevents the state from favouring some at the expense of others. The second introduces the notion of equality as a political objective: levelling out existing differences by introducing compensatory differences. The third seeks out the particularity of each situation in order to offer the most appropriate response to its possibilities, whether these are positive or negative. But each of these logics also has its dark side The first conceals social injustices. The second creates new injustices in correcting old ones. The third subsumes justice in a more or less random series of individual cases" (my translation). Some of these problems are examined below.

11 The inclusion of sex was a brilliant accident. The measure was designed originally only to prohibit race discrimination. An amendment to include sex discrimination, intended to make the Bill a laughing stock, was moved and passed; and so was the Bill as amended.

adverse impact—perhaps deliberate, perhaps accidental—on one sex or racial group. Early in the now chequered existence of the Civil Rights Act the Supreme Court ruled:

> "Congress has now provided that tests or criteria for employment or promotion may not provide equality of opportunity merely in the sense of the fabled offer of milk to the stork and the fox. . . . It has . . . provided that the vessel in which the milk is proffered be one all seekers can use".[12]

The Sex Discrimination Act 1975 and the Race Relations Act 1976, leaving nothing to chance in the manner of British drafting, spelt out the analytical process by which indirect discrimination was to be identified and, if identified, justified.[13] The formula can be problematical to apply, but over time it has worked, not only in courts and tribunals but—far more importantly—by changing good practice so as to replace subjective and undisciplined recruitment procedures with relevant job and personal criteria designed to find the best candidate.

But neither law nor practice has succeeded in eliminating inequality of opportunity for ethnic minorities and women; nor will it, in some fields at least, unless entrenched forms of elitism, most of them based on inherited and unarticulated assumptions, are directly challenged. The powerful case in some of these fields for affirmative action—that is to say, for loading the criteria of choice in favour of those who have historically been disadvantaged—encounters the equally powerful argument that if discrimination on grounds of race or sex is wrong, then doing it for benign reasons cannot make it right. It also encounters the practical argument that, while affirmative action to encourage disadvantaged groups to come forward is acceptable, positive discrimination by definition involves a selective dilution of standards. These arguments, built as they are on the very legislation which sets out to combat discrimination,

---

12 *Griggs v. Duke Power Co.* 401 U.S. 424 (1971), *per* Burger C.J. for the Court at 431. (The reference is to Aesop's fable of the fox who offers the crane a drink in a flat dish and is offered in return by the crane a drink from a long-necked flagon.) The European Court of Justice has taken the same course in construing the Equal Treatment Directive: see case 170/84 *Bilka-Kaufhaus GMBH v. Weber von Harz* [1986] E.C.R. 1607.

13 Sex Discrimination Act 1975, s. 1(1). *cf* Race Relations Act 1976, s. 1(1): "A person discriminates against a woman . . . if . . . (b) he applies to her a requirement or condition which applies or would apply equally to a man but (i) which is such that the proportion of women who can comply with it is considerably smaller than the proportion of men who can comply with it, and (ii) which he cannot show to be justifiable irrespective of the sex of the person to whom it is applied, and (iii) which is to her detriment because she cannot comply with it."

seem to have a monopoly of justice: how, they ask, can you combat discrimination by discriminating? Yet history argues differently. History shows us centuries of positive discrimination in favour of white men: of jobs and advantages going to incompetent and mediocrities whose faces happened to fit or who had the right connections. It helps to explain why forms of inequality remain embedded in our ways of thinking and operating. Women and members of ethnic minorities still face real problems of self-confidence in even deciding to try to enter fields of activity where the white male image dominates. And for those who do enter, experience still suggests that those who succeed have to do better than their white male counterparts. As a society we continue, for the present at least, to set our faces against practices which will turn these tables. We accept the legitimacy of target numbers against which to monitor performance; but we do not allow the use of quotas to redress performance which is proving inadequate. The consequent near-stalemate is a different but no less real form of injustice. We have legislated against individual acts of discrimination, for each of which the law can try to provide a remedy; but we have no legal means of dealing with the kinds of systemic disadvantage that the legislation has so far failed to reverse. One marginal solution, within the present law, is to prioritise those relevant criteria of choice which members of disadvantaged minorities are more likely to be able to satisfy. Another, now adopted in such countries as Canada and New Zealand, is to keep a quota of places for historically disadvantaged minorities in institutions—chiefly universities—which provide the passkeys to the problem areas of employment, housing and so on.[14]

These are entirely defensible, albeit contested, legal policy initiatives. But they throw up a succession of further questions. If the number of university places is finite, for everybody who is admitted somebody is excluded. It may be law's task to say what are the permitted and what are the forbidden criteria of choice, but in making the distinction legislatures, and judges in

---

14 In Canada the key provision is section 15 of the Charter of Rights and Freedoms 1982, which by subsection (1) guarantees the equal protection of the law without discrimination, but by subsection (2) provides: "Subsection (1) does not preclude any law, programme or activity that has as its object the amelioration of conditions of disadvantaged individuals or groups . . . ". In New Zealand the Human Rights Act 1983, s. 73, makes analogous provision; but in relation to Maori it may be that the necessary authority is in Article II of the Treaty of Waitangi. The Constitution of South Africa, s. 9(2), provides: "Equality includes the full and equal enjoyment of all rights and freedoms. To promote the achievement of equality, legislative and other measures designed to protect or advance persons, or categories of persons, disadvantaged by unfair discrimination may be taken."

43

their wake, have to make fundamental decisions about justice. They must choose, in particular, between immediate justice to individuals and long-term justice to segments of society—not because of some inherent superiority of group over individual, but precisely because the typecasting of many individual members of a group may make it necessary to take remedial steps on behalf of the group in order to liberate the individuals who compose it.

There is a powerful argument that judges, if they are to do justice, ought to resort to principle rather than to precedent in deciding difficult cases.[15] But the argument only begins here. The question it repeatedly begs is: what principle? There are issues, of which affirmative action and positive discrimination are one, on which fundamentally different positions of principle can legitimately be taken. Ronald Dworkin has persuasively defended reverse discrimination both on the grounds of concern and respect which inform his theory of justice and on utilitarian grounds.[16] But principles, as he acknowledges, can be misappropriated. How would we react if the principle upon which Dworkin defends selection criteria designed to redress the under-representation of blacks in American law schools were used to reduce a real or supposed over-representation of Jews? The issue, which Dworkin himself recognises, illustrates something which triumphalist talk about justice ignores: that even from a single broad standpoint there may well be more than one just outcome, and that the choice between just outcomes may itself raise questions of fundamental principle which cannot be resolved without resort to philosophical and political premises which ordinarily lie beyond the judicial remit. In the kind of case I have taken, for example, the underlying decisions which have to be made are between social and moral evils which have somehow to be first quantified and then compared. In other cases the law finds itself trapped between inherited assumptions of the kind I mentioned earlier and a developing social morality: can there be rape within marriage?[17] what beneficial interest does a non-earning spouse have in the matrimonial home?[18]

---

15 For a wide-ranging and powerful argument to this effect, see Hon. E.W. Thomas, "A return to principle in judicial reasoning and an acclamation of judicial autonomy", Victoria University of Wellington Law Review monograph (1983). I considered in the previous lecture some of the common law's reasons for using precedent as a golden thread in the maze.
16 Ronald Dworkin, *Taking Rights Seriously* (1977), chap. 9.
17 See *R. v. R.* [1992] 1 A.C. 599.
18 See *Gissing v. Gissing* [1971] A.C. 886, endorsing a quasi-contractual approach through property rights and "common intent"; *cf Cooke v. Head* [1972] 1 W.L.R. 519, seeking a better solution through trust law.

do parents have a right to beat their children?[19] does sovereign immunity extend to perpetrators of crimes against humanity?[20] The courts in such situations have choices of principle to make—between the injustice of deciding that the law is not what it was thought to be and the injustice of tolerating something that has become or is becoming intolerable. Although there are principles of fairness which limit the choice—for example that a change in the law may not criminalise what was an innocent act when it was done,[21] nor destroy vested rights[22]—there remains a large area governed in the last resort only by the courts' receptivity or resistance to change. And because the courts decide only real cases, not abstract questions, there is superimposed the problem that the just solution of a hard case may make law which produces fresh and unexpected injustices in other cases. It is not a sufficient response to this familiar problem to counsel endless judicial caution by reciting the adage that hard cases make bad law; bad law makes hard cases too.

The rhetoric of the law should not obscure the fact that justice—of process as much as of outcome—is in large part a matter of personal perception. What justice a legal system achieves is more likely to be a negotiated outcome with rough edges and loose ends than a triumphal result pronounced to universal acclaim. And the complication of justice is added to by disparities of access. With the coming of the Human Rights Act one can venture some predictions, based both on experience to date in this country[23] and on the experience of Canada under its 1982 Charter of Rights and Freedoms and of New Zealand under its Bill of Rights Act 1990. One is that when—at a date which is not likely to be before the middle of the year 2000—the human rights shop opens, that endlessly indignant litigant, the drinking driver, will be waiting there. He will be hoping to follow the trail blazed early in the life of the Charter by his Canadian counterpart, who was stopped by the police at 3 a.m. in sub-zero conditions, well inside the Arctic Circle and went to court to assert that the right to counsel entitled him not to have to blow into the bag until his lawyer had been brought several hundred miles from

19 See most recently the decision of the European Court of Human Rights in A. v. U.K. [1998] E.H.R.L.R. 82.
20 *R. v. Bartle, ex p. Pinochet* [1998] 3 W.L.R. 1456; March 24, 1999.
21 See the European Convention on Human Rights, Art. 7.
22 See F.A. Bennion, *Statutory Interpretation* (3rd ed.), s. 97.
23 From *Sunday Times v. U.K.* (1979) 2 E.H.R.R. 245 to *R. v. Home Secretary, ex p. Brind*]1991] 1 A.C. 696.

Whitehorse.[24] Another (I don't mean to put the two on a par) is that litigation about freedom of expression under Article 10 of the Convention will be near or at the head of the queue. Why should it be so?

Since anybody who even asks such a question risks being branded an enemy of free speech, let me first reiterate[25] that the right to utter criticism or heresy without fear of suppression or reprisal from those who may be angered or embarrassed by it is fundamental in any free society. But other rights are no less important. Why does experience suggest that they tend to be less frequently and less stridently claimed? May the disparity have to do with disparities of power? Is it the lion who litigates while the ox puts up with things? Access to the courts is expensive, but for those organisations which possess and depend for their prosperity on audibility, inhibitions on what they can say are important enough to justify investment in rights litigation. We are likely to see commercial interests prominent among those claiming the right of free expression in relation to the advertising of things which government wants to regulate.[26] Differences in financial muscle may also have a considerable influence upon what is made in our courts of a particular scheduled right. Article 8[27] claims, for example, may quite rapidly establish a rich jurisprudence of privacy rights for the famous.[28] They are far less likely to do so for the larger number of humble people whose autonomy is endlessly compromised by a variety of processes to which public administration subjects them as claimants, clients or patients. For them, legal advice is not readily available and legal aid, limited now by means testing to the poorest, is likely to be the only route to court. For the middling sort in the coming period real problems are likely to be encoun-

24 See now, in the Supreme Court of Canada, *R. v. Bartle* [1994] 35 S.C.R. 173; in the New Zealand Court of Appeal, *Ministry of Transport v. Noort* [1992] 3 N.Z.L.R. 260.
25 See S. Sedley, "The First Amendment: a case for import controls?" in I. Loveland ed., *Importing the First Amendment* (1998), p. 24.
26 *cf* the problems posed to and by the Canadian Supreme Court in relation to cigarette advertising: *RJR MacDonald Inc.* [1995] 3 S.C.R. 199.
27 Article 8 provides: (1) Everyone has the right to respect for his private and family life, his home and his correspondence. (2) There shall be no interference by a public authority with the exercise of this right except such as is in accordance with the law and is necessary in a democratic society in the interests of national security, public safety or the economic wellbeing of the country, for the prevention of disorder or crime, for the protection of health or morals, or for the protection of the rights and freedoms of others.
28 The case for the development of a law of privacy under the umbrella of Article 8 is touched on in the second lecture. It is fair to point out, however, that the doors opened by media corporations in free speech cases are doors through which others may pass.

tered in finding lawyers who are prepared—or indeed finan-
cially able—to work for contingent fees on human rights
issues.[29] It may be for this reason, rather than as a reflection
of the real incidence of Convention issues, that criminal law,
where legal aid remains available as of right, will initially at
least become the arena of the most numerous human rights
arguments.

Why should any of this matter? Why is the market in litigation
not itself a sufficient indicator of need? Law-and-economics
theory, at least in its early versions, might well claim that it
is.[30] Communitarian theories, on the other hand, begin by posit-
ing fairness in the distribution of individual rights or freedoms
as the essence of justice. To speak of justice, of course, is not
necessarily to speak of law: the judicial job is to achieve the one
in applying the other, but the rigidity of law and the elusiveness
of justice continually conspire to keep the two things in tension.
If, as I have argued, there is frequently no single just outcome to
a particular conflict, justice itself requires the possibility of non-
confrontational forms of conflict resolution; and the courts
themselves are starting to recognise and promote mediation
as a sometimes better route to justice. But to the extent that
courts of law, with their confrontational processes, remain the
forum in which justice is ordinarily sought, it is (or so it seems
to me) from a common ethical sense rather than from any
prescriptive or functional source that justice as a value embody-
ing fairness and equity has to be derived. Neither Rawls[31] nor
Dworkin[32] can prove *why* it is justice in this sense that matters;
nor need they so long as we endorse the moral sensibility
which says that it does. It is perhaps significant that in an era
when equality in other fields has either imploded or been
exploded as a guiding ideal, equality before the law remains
an uncontested good and an unchallenged right. Is there in the
end an element of human sensibility which, because it is as
much aesthetic as it is moral, is unsatisfied with an outcome
loaded by extraneous factors which skew the creative acts of
debate and judgment by which justice is done and displayed?[33]
Whatever the reason, we continue to want the forensic playing
field to be level.

29 See (at the time of writing) *Modernising Justice: the Government's plans for
reforming legal services and the courts* (Cm. 4155, December 1998), ch. 3.
30 See A. Ogus, "Law and Economics from the Perspective of Law" in P. Newman
ed., *The New Palgrave Dictionary of Law and Economics* (1998), Vol. 2, p. 486.
31 John Rawls, *A Theory of Justice* (1971).
32 Ronald Dworkin, *Taking Rights Seriously* (1977).
33 Perhaps the title of Geoffrey Robertson's book, *The Justice Game* (1998), gives
the clue.

This is more easily said than done. It is not simply that some witnesses give a poorer account of themselves than others when they may well be the more truthful; nor that the quality of legal representation may unfairly favour one party, whether by chance or by purchase. It is that the legal process is itself based on assumptions which can turn procedures designed to achieve evenhandedness into engines of oppression. I will take two examples, one procedural and one substantive.

It is a central principle of our criminal procedure that the defence must be allowed to explore the weaknesses in the Crown's case and to put its own case without inhibition. A rape case is in principle a criminal trial like any other, but in practice it has been known for a long time that unless the process is controlled a rape trial will as often as not be turned into a trial of the complainant. It is thanks largely to the fact that women have made themselves heard over the last 30 years or so that Parliament and the courts have tried in some measure to reverse this process. But the consequent statutory presumption against questioning a complainant about her sexual past, which is necessarily rebuttable if justice requires it in a particular case, has turned out to provide uneven and sometimes illusory protection.[34]

What is more, the adversarial process itself can obstruct rather than promote justice. This is well recognised by the family courts, which have long since taken charge of the evidential process in order to ensure that on marriage breakdown the children are not fought over like property along with the house and the car, and that in abuse cases the court decides what is safest for the child, not who wins. Other branches of civil process lag behind; and the criminal process remains trapped in a body of rules which at times seem more apt to a game of snakes and ladders than to a system of justice. Many of the problems are highlighted in rape cases, but rape cases are not special: they simply tend to show in particularly acute form some of the anomalies of the adversarial system in the form which history and culture have given it in England and Wales.

A rape case will typically involve a young woman whose lifestyle is somewhere between the casual and the chaotic, and a young man who has found her in this situation and has forced himself on her.[35] With the coming of DNA testing, the "It wasn't

---

34 Sexual Offences (Amendment) Act 1976, s.2, as construed in *R. v. Lawrence* [1977] Crim. L.R. 492, *viz* that such cross-examination should be allowed where it "might reasonably lead the jury . . . to take a different view of the complainant's evidence . . .".

35 A disturbing proportion of these defendants turns out to have been acquitted of one or more rapes in similar circumstances in the past.

me" defence has almost disappeared. The defence will be that the complainant consented, and it will more often than not be cast in pornographic detail which presents her as the initiator. The first the victim is likely to learn of these counter-allegations is when, having told the jury her story, the defendant's counsel gets up to cross-examine her. Although attention has in recent times been focused on defendants who dismiss their counsel and cross-examine in person, the experience of crucifixion by a skilled and remorseless advocate can be even worse. The very vulnerabilities which made the complainant prey to the defendant in the first place now make her a prey to the barrister and to the more censorious of the jurors: why was she not living at home? why was she out at 2 a.m.? why did she allow the defendant to be alone with her? We have simply not been able to reconcile the need to ensure that an accused person is not wrongly convicted with the equally important need to protect the complainant from becoming the accused in a counter-trial about her lifestyle. Judges no doubt become case-hardened: many of us have heard this kind of defence so often that we could script it ourselves. We know too that a high proportion of these men have access to offender networks (especially but not exclusively in prison[36]) where defences which place the victim in the dock are circulated. The jury is an essential protection against the consequent risk of typecasting defendants; but because each jury is hearing the story for the first and only time there is an opposite risk that, having no objective evidence such as injuries (and these are the exception in rape cases), and not knowing how consistently consent defences are manufactured, they will accept that the defence might be true and will acquit. Nobody can say in any one case that they are wrong to do so; but experience tells one with near-certainty that the low and still falling rate of conviction in rape cases[37] reflects a systemic injustice to those women who in disturbing numbers fall victim to predatory men.

The task of achieving fairness between accuser and accused in such cases rests not only on the trial judge but on the trial advocate. There *are* counsel—many of them—who can put their client's case and test the Crown's evidence without compromise but equally without insult or injury. There are others—a small but prominent minority—who either cannot

36 Such contact and exchange of defences is made even easier by the Home Office's need to segregate sex offenders, whether convicted or on remand, for their own protection under Rule 43 of the Prison Rules.
37 J. Harris, *The Processing of Rape Cases by the Criminal Justice System*: interim report (1997), unpublished, Home Office.

or will not do so,[38] and with these the trial judge has a herculean task in preventing the humiliation and bullying of the complainant[39] without provoking a successful appeal on the ground that the defence was prevented from putting its case. In my view the initiative and the responsibility at present rest with the Bar. There is no longer a place for a forensic culture which tolerates and even promotes something closer to bare-knuckle fighting than to a fair trial and a quest for a just verdict, and which fails to insist upon advocacy which treats with respect individuals, the good, the bad and the ugly alike, who find themselves in the temporary but overwhelming power of an interrogator in a wig. There is no worthwhile evidence that inquisitorial systems are intrinsically better or fairer; but it does not follow that they are without virtues, or that an adversarial system has to demean and oppress those who get caught up in it. Fairness in a trial concerns more people than the accused.[40]

It is perhaps in the criminal sentencing process that justice comes under the cruellest spotlight. It is not simply that almost every sentence except one prescribed by law is a compromise between justice to the wrongdoer and justice to the victim, or between such incommensurable imperatives as reform and retribution; nor simply that the law which continues to prescribe a life sentence for every murder is itself an impossible compromise between justice and vengeance. Nor is it simply that public comprehension of sentencing has been so damaged by media presentation that the public simultaneously believe that judges sentence too leniently and, when asked concretely what they would do, turn out to favour sentences markedly lighter than judges in fact impose.[41] It is that we continue to be both fasci-

38 Recent research by Jennifer Temkin has elicited an alarming disparity between the Bar's Code of Conduct, which forbids the asking of questions which mere vilify or annoy, and the admitted (indeed boasted) use by counsel of vilification as a routine tactic in rape cases (Lecture, "Justice in Rape Trials", October 27, 1998; publication forthcoming).

39 The Royal Commission on Criminal Justice (1993) considered this an important but neglected part of the judicial role: see its Report (Cm. 2263) Chap. 8, para. 12.

40 For a valuable critical analysis of the adversarial process see Jenny McEwan, *Evidence and the Adversarial Process* (2nd ed., 1998). Louise Ellison's article "Cross-examination in rape trials" [1998] Crim. L.R. 605 supports the view that the faults of rape trials are the faults of criminal process and of the Bar writ large. Her footnotes furnish an up-to-date bibliography of the subject.

41 M. Hough and J. Roberts, *Attitudes to Punishment: findings from the British Crime Survey* (Home Office Research Study 179, 1998). The question whether insistent media misinformation has been taken for public opinion and has led to sentence inflation during the 1990s is an important one which needs to be more fully addressed than I can do here.

nated and baffled by the interplay between compulsion and freewill.

The law starts from an assumption that people are responsible for what they do in the sense that they can choose not to do it. It has for centuries made it a principle that "a man cannot stultify himself" by excusing what he has done on grounds of his own fecklessness or incapacity.[42] It abandons this position for those who are incapable of knowing what they are doing, or that what they are doing is wrong,[43] or whose acts or minds are for one reason or another—intoxication excepted[44]—not their own.[45] For those who, though criminally responsible, are mentally disturbed it provides specialised disposals at the point of sentencing.[46] But this leaves a vast number of cases—the majority, indeed—in which a defendant may have been driven by something inside or outside him- or herself to offend. For thieves it may be need, genuine or perceived; for sexual abusers it is commonly a history of having themselves been abused; frequently in mugging and burglary cases it is the compulsion to feed a drug addiction; and as frequently in cases of violence it is the short fuse of anger. The law is on the whole uncompromising in holding people responsible for what they do under such pressure (with the notable exception of the law of homicide, which uniquely allows provocation to afford a defence, reducing murder to manslaughter with a quantum drop in the penalty). Justice for its part, in the form of sentence, can sometimes show mercy but cannot dilute the principle of responsibility.

For a long time this moral, even moralistic, view has sat awkwardly beside the belief that criminality, far from being a matter of choice, is an aspect of personality—in its cruder forms a function of heredity discernible in the shape of the skull.[47]

---

42 *Beverley's Case* (1603) 4 Co. Rep. 123b.
43 *M'Naghten's Case* (1843) 10 Cl. & F 200.
44 *R. v. Majewski* [1977] A.C. 443.
45 *DPP for N Ireland v. Lynch* [1975] A.C. 653; *quaere* whether the intellectual basis of duress can coexist with the decision of the House of Lords in *R. v. Kingston* [1995] 2 A.C. 355 in relation to intoxication.
46 Mental Health Act 1983, s. 37 (hospital orders); Powers of Criminal Courts Act 1973, Sched. 1A, para. 5 (probation with a condition of treatment).
47 The endurance of the belief that personality is written in physique is remarkable when one reflects how false daily experience proves it to be. Is Lombroso's phrenologically challenged recidivist more than a post-Darwinian version of Richard III?:

> "I that am curtailed of this fair proportion,
> Cheated of feature by dissembling nature,
> Deformed, unfinished, sent before my time
> Into this breathing world scarce half made up . . .

While deductions have ranged from eugenic final solutions to arguments for the abolition of imprisonment, the one thing that theories of entrenched criminality cannot sustain is the belief that prison works, except by way of temporary containment. If prison is to reform (and our Prison Rules have since 1899 announced this as the primary purpose of imprisonment) it can only be because offenders are capable of changing their behaviour. Yet day after day realistic and thoughtful pre-sentence reports confront sentencing courts with desperate portraits of individuals irreparably damaged by their formative experiences. The court knows, as it sends them down, that it is in a sense punishing them again for what life has already done to them; yet it also knows, or believes, that without a condign response society risks losing its already contested grip on civil order and the courts their toehold in public confidence; and so we continue to hold them responsible for what they have done.

This constant negotiation of the meaning of justice is going to find itself under new pressures in the coming generation. The feedback of the reductionist Darwinism most strongly associated in this country with "selfish gene" theory[48] has not simply been a (surely unintended) endorsement of a particular strain of individualist ideology. By encouraging determinist ideas about human behaviour it has reinvigorated the notion that anti-social conduct can be both appropriate and desirable—more appropriate and desirable than the artifical construct of human society.[49] It also challenges received notions of freedom and freewill, not necessarily by presenting the human being as a genetically programmed automaton, but by postulating selfish ends as the "natural" objectives of the free individual.

You cannot meet a scientific case of this kind by resisting its

> And therefore since I cannot prove a lover
> To entertain these fair well-spoken days,
> I am determined to prove a villain . . . "

What may be far more to the point is that the mockery and bullying to which children with peculiarities are subjected by their peers and, sometimes, by adults may well have an enduring impact on their behaviour and their attitude to others. For a developed society, our comprehension of cause and effect is slender.

48 Richard Dawkins, *The Selfish Gene* (1976); *The Blind Watchmaker* (1986). The hazards of his method emerge sharply from well-known passage from the latter book about rain falling on a growing tree: "It is raining DNA . . . It is raining instructions out there . . . That is not a metaphor, it is the plain truth. It couldn't be any plainer if it were raining floppy discs."

49 An example in recent years has been the "Guiness defence" in fraud cases: the prosecution establishes the illegality or impropriety of a commercial practice, and the defence (to negative dishonesty) then calls a string of respectable witnesses to say that everybody does it.

conclusions on moral or political grounds. What matters is the scientific critique of it as a monist grand theory which can make its case only by denying the demonstrable complexity and indeterminacy of the natural world, starting with the dependence of the genetic material itself upon the functioning of the cell which holds it[50] and extending to the very nature of matter and of life.[51] The human reality which the law both encounters and is part of has at least the virtue of mimicking this infinitely complicated and labile universe, ultimately explicable but lacking any single determinant. Such a reality may close down the anticipation of a short and easy solution to the problem of crime, as it does to the problem of life, but understanding it will continue to bring us closer to some understanding of the multiplex sources of human conduct. The presently attractive evidence that there is a genetic component in certain forms of behaviour does not spell an end to responsibility or freewill; but it does have implications both for the symbiosis of justice and mercy and for the dilemma of reform and containment.[52]

In quite different ways, too, changes in society's material potentiality are likely to impact on legal values. Thanks chiefly to medical advances we have a rapidly ageing population in the developed countries: people are living longer and having fewer children. The pattern of dependency in a generation's time is going to place new and alarming pressures not only on ethical but on legal assumptions about something as fundamental, and now as entrenched in our law, as the right to life. The courts have already determined that the allocation of interventionist medical resources, even where life is at stake, is ordinarily not justiciable[53]; but how long will it be before a foundering medical service asks whether it can withdraw first medical attention and then nourishment from incurably demented geriatric patients? If it happens, will the courts do what they did (and did with

50 See Steven Rose, *Lifelines* (1997), p. 131.
51 The American palaeontologist Stephen Jay Gould is perhaps the best-known contemporary exponent of a non-linear and non-determinist theory of evolution (see *Life's Grandeur* (1996)). The misnamed chaos theory—in fact a theory of causation in the ostensibly random—continues to contribute in a variety of fields to this approach. The Gaia theory of a self-adjusting planet made an earlier contribution to it (James Lovelock, *Gaia: a New Look at Life on Earth* (1979)).
52 See Steven Rose, "Neuroscience, responsibility and the law" (paper given to the Howard League for Penal Reform, September 1998). The debate in turn suggests questions about our own values: how is it, for example, that some of the indicia used by occupational psychologists to identify aggression (a strong plus factor in the recruitment of executives) are the same indicia as those used by psychiatrists to identify paranoid personality disorder?
53 *R. v. Cambridge Health Authority, ex p. B* [1995] 1 W.L.R. 398, CA.

distinction) in Tony Bland's case[54] and decide something because Parliament would decide nothing?[55] If they do, by what legal and ethical standards will they answer the question? It is one of history's ironies that, having now put the judicial taking of life behind us, the law's ability to sanction the taking, or more urgently the non-prolongation, of life by others is likely to come dramatically to the fore. But less dramatically too, for example in relation to the enforcement of living wills: for who is to know whether any one of us, signing away our continued existence in the event of incurable degenerative illness at a time when we are fit and confident, would have been saying the same when that point was reached? In matters of life and death the law has ahead of it a fraught journey ahead which is going to jolt our notions of justice.

But, the problem is not just ahead of us: homelessness is here and now. In my second lecture I mentioned some of the things which are not to be found in the European Convention of Human Rights, among them a right to shelter. The ideal of negative liberty, which I touched on in the first lecture, has little to offer the homeless: they are as unconstrained by law as the next person, and so long as nobody is interfering with them they are free. If, however, you ask the question which I have suggested the common law (and almost any model of justice I can think of) would ask, namely "free to do what?", the answer is almost nothing. Possibly they are encouraged by the fact that an Act of Parliament now protects their right to hold up a piece of card saying "Hungry and homeless", for this is the right of free expression protected by Article 10 of the Convention. But beyond this the homeless are, as has been well said, comprehensively unfree.[56] Their legal liberty to seek work and to rent accommodation has reached a dead end, and they are free only to sleep rough. Why should it matter to them that they live under the rule of law? One of my enduring images from early days in metropolitan magistrates' courts is the down-and-out who has thrown a brick through a shop window on Christmas Eve so that he can at least be housed and fed in custody on Christmas Day.

This kind of Dickensian sentiment, true, is easy enough to conjure up. It has to do, no doubt, with social justice, but does it have anything to do with the justice administered by the

---

54 *Airedale NHS Trust v. Bland* [1973] A.C. 789.
55 I have commented on this situation in M. Nolan and S. Sedley, *The Making and Remaking of the British Constitution* (1997), pp. 57–58.
56 Jeremy Waldron, "Homelessness and the issue of freedom" 39 U.C.L.A. Law Rev. 295 at 302 (1991).

courts? In my view it does, for neither justice nor law necessarily requires a formal foundation in tabulated rights. The pure economic liberal view, indeed, is that rights do not come into the picture at all: Hayek, for example, argues that unless the creation of misery is deliberate, poverty involves no injustice.[57] It must equally be the case from a communitarian standpoint that a practical limit exists to what rights the courts can enforce against the state, especially where the right to litigate belongs only to individuals. A successful legal claim—for recognition of special educational or physical needs, for instance—may simply mean reallocating already inadequate funds within a ring-fenced local budget, so that the silent pay for the gains of the assertive.

If injustice there is then, it lies deeper than the allocation or denial of rights—dependence on which, as my colleague John Laws has argued, is in a sense a sign of an immature society.[58] It has to do with what I have suggested earlier in this lecture is a common sense of equity, an ethic of kindness, a morality of feeling, which does not and cannot be expected to stop at a desire for legal justice, even though that is necessarily where the law itself must stop. But within the law's necessary limits I see nothing wrong with the reaction of a good judge of recent years, Mr Justice McKenna, when in my early years at the Bar he was asked to grant injunctions ordering some travellers to leave a roadside verge to which they had been forcibly removed from other land. "Where are they to go?" he asked. "That's not our concern," said the local authority's counsel, "We're entitled to an order". "These are human beings," said McKenna, "And you're not getting any order until you can tell me where they are to go." It may be beyond the power of the courts to change a world in

---

57 F.A. Hayek, *Law, Legislation and Liberty: the Mirage of Social Justice* (1976), quoted by Waldron, *op. cit.*: "It has of course to be admitted that the manner in which the benefits and burdens are apportioned by the market mechanism would in many instances have to be regarded as very unjust *if* it were the result of a deliberate allocation to particular people. But this is not the case. Those shares are the outcome of a process the effect of which on particular people was neither intended nor foreseen by anyone." Comment is superfluous, but the trickle-down effect of Hayek's thinking, through the Chicago-based early law-and-economics movement, has been paralleled by versions of sociobiology which use the same monetarist mathematical models. These in turn have sought to influence criminology; they have also been borrowed back, in a way which may give pause to Dawkins' readers, by monetarists in the form of "evolutionary economics". See Rose, *op. cit.* (n. 50 ante), p. 53.

58 Sir John Laws, "The limitations of human rights" [1998] P.P.L. 254 at 255: "As it seems to me the idea of a *rights-based* society represents an immature stage in the development of a free and just society . . . . A society whose values are defined by reference to individual rights is by that very fact already impoverished. Its culture says nothing about individual duty—nothing about *virtue*."

which privation in the midst of plenty is possible; but that does not mean that they are obliged to endorse all the consequent injustices.[59]

Lord Reid once observed that people want the law to be two incompatible things—certain and adaptable.[60] Lord Atkin knew which was the more important: "Finality is a good thing," he said, "but justice is a better."[61] I have suggested in the course of these lectures that the idea of a free society as a condition of individual freedom is an integral and still relevant part of our historical legacy; that law in a free and moral society, while it is not its job to redistribute power, is concerned centrally with the abuse of power wherever it resides; and that justice has to be sought not in some crystalline outcome but as a process of principled negotiation through law of interests which may be no less legitimate for want of the status of tabulated rights. It is a long way, I know, from Sir Alfred Denning's lucid and persuasive account in the first Hamlyn Lectures of a society and a legal system which, in spite of occasional problems, had basically got it right. Half a century on, as it seems to me, we have a lot to be glad of and a lot to build on, but also much still to worry about and, with luck and judgment, to resolve.

---

59 "Mais où s'arreter, lorsqu'on s'engage dans cette voie d'ajustement à la marge? Et comment respecter l'égalité, éviter l'arbitraire, échapper à la confusion?" ("But where do you stop once you have started on this path of marginal adjustment? And how do you maintain equality, avoid arbitrariness and escape confusion?"): Guy Braibant, "Nouvelles reflexions sur les rapports du droit et de l'équité", *Revue française d'administration publique*, no. 64, p. 691. In other words, the problem of the hard case is always there.

60 Lord Reid, "The Judge as Law-maker" (1972) 12 J.S.P.T.L. 22.

61 *Ras Behari Lal v. King-Emperor* (1933) 50 T.L.R. 1.

INDEX

Index

58

Index